T5-AEU-859

WITHDRAWN FROM
KENT STATE UNIVERSITY LIBRARIES

ACCOUNTABILITY IN PRACTICE

Other titles in the Cassell Education series:

P. Ainley: *Young People Leaving Home*

P. Ainley and M. Corney: *Training for the Future: The Rise and Fall of the Manpower Services Commission*

G. Allen and I. Martin (eds): *Education and Community: The Politics of Practice*

G. Antonouris and J. Wilson: *Equal Opportunities in Schools: New Dimensions in Topic Work*

M. Barber: *Education in the Capital*

L. Bash and D. Coulby: *The Education Reform Act: Competition and Control*

D.E. Bland: *Managing Higher Education*

M. Booth, J. Furlong and M. Wilkin: *Partnership in Initial Teacher Training*

M. Bottery: *The Morality of the School*

G. Claxton: *Being a Teacher: A Positive Approach to Change and Stress*

G. Claxton: *Teaching to Learn: A Direction for Education*

D. Coffey: *Schools and Work: Developments in Vocational Education*

D. Coulby and L. Bash: *Contradiction and Conflict: The 1988 Education Act in Action*

D. Coulby and S. Ward (eds): *The Primary Core National Curriculum*

L.B. Curzon: *Teaching in Further Education* (4th edition)

P. Daunt: *Meeting Disability: A European Response*

J. Freeman: *Gifted Children Growing Up*

J. Lynch: *Education for Citizenship in a Multicultural Society*

J. Nias, G. Southworth and R. Yeomans: *Staff Relationships in the Primary School*

A. Pollard and S. Tann: *Reflective Teaching in the Primary School* (2nd edition)

R. Ritchie (ed.): *Profiling in Primary Schools: A Handbook for Teachers*

A. Rogers: *Adults Learning for Development*

B. Spiecker and R. Straughan (eds): *Freedom and Indoctrination in Education: International Perspectives*

A. Stables: *An Approach to English*

R. Straughan: *Beliefs, Behaviour and Education*

M. Styles, E. Bearne and V. Watson (eds): *After Alice: Exploring Children's Literature*

S. Tann: *Developing Language in the Primary Classroom*

H. Thomas: *Education Costs and Performance*

H. Thomas with G. Kirkpatrick and E. Nicholson: *Financial Delegation and the Local Management of Schools*

D. Thyer: *Mathematical Enrichment Exercises: A Teacher's Guide*

D. Thyer and J. Maggs: *Teaching Mathematics to Young Children* (3rd edition)

M. Watts: *The Science of Problem-solving*

M. Watts (ed.): *Science in the National Curriculum*

J. Wilson: *A New Introduction to Moral Education*

S. Wolfendale *et al.* (eds): *The Profession and Practice of Educational Psychology: Future Directions*

Accountability in Practice

John Lello

CASSELL

Cassell
Villiers House   387 Park Avenue South
41/47 Strand   New York
London WC2N 5JE   NY 10016-8810

ⓒ John Lello 1993

All rights reserved. No part of this publication may be reproduced or transmitted
in any form or by any means, electronic or mechanical including photocopying,
recording or any information storage or retrieval system, without prior permission
in writing from the publishers.

First published 1993

British Library Cataloguing-in-Publication Data
A catalogue record for this book is available from the British Library.

ISBN 0-304-32748-4 (hardback)
      0-304-32740-9 (paperback)

Typeset by Colset Private Limited, Singapore
Printed and bound in Great Britain by
Biddles Ltd, Guildford and King's Lynn

Contents

Abbreviations

ACAS	Advisory, Conciliation and Arbitration Service
AGIT	Action for Governors' Information and Training
AMMA	Assistant Masters' and Mistresses' Association
APA	accreditation of prior achievement
APL	accreditation of prior learning
CASE	Campaign for the Advancement of State Education
CNAA	Council for National Academic Awards
CTC	City Technology College
DES	Department of Education and Science
DfE	Department for Education
GCSE	General Certificate of Secondary Education
GM	grant-maintained (school)
HEFC	Higher Education Funding Council
HMA	Head Masters Association
HMC	Headmasters' Conference
HMI	Her Majesty's Inspector *or* Her Majesty's Inspectorate
IB	International Baccalaureate
Inlogov	Institute of Local Government Studies
ISCG	Institute of School and College Governors
ISIS	Independent Schools Information Service
LEA	local education authority
LMS	local management of schools
NAGM	National Association of Governors and Managers
NAHT	National Association of Head Teachers

NALGO	National and Local Government Officers Association
NAS/UWT	National Association of Schoolmasters/Union of Women Teachers
NCC	National Curriculum Council
NCPTA	National Confederation of Parent–Teacher Associations
NCVQ	National Council for Vocational Qualifications
NUT	National Union of Teachers
OECD	Organization for Economic Co-operation and Development
OFSTED	Office for Standards in Education
PCFC	Polytechnics and Colleges Funding Council
PGCE	Postgraduate Certificate in Education
PRP	performance-related pay
SCAA	School Curriculum and Assessment Authority
SEAC	School Examinations and Assessment Council
SHA	Secondary Heads Association
SORP	Statement of Recommended Practice
TES	*Times Educational Supplement*
THES	*Times Higher Educational Supplement*
TVEI	Technical and Vocational Education Initiative
UFC	Universities Funding Council
UGC	University Grants Committee
YTS	Youth Training Scheme

The whole theory of modern education is radically unsound. Fortunately in England, at any rate, education produces no effect whatsoever. If it did, it would prove a serious danger to the upper classes.

Lady Bracknell, in *The Importance of Being Earnest* (1895) by Oscar Wilde

Chapter 1

Meaning and Interpretation

Accountability 'involves reporting to other people voluntarily or compulsorily. It means having a conscience or a moral responsibility about what you are doing. It means being answerable to other people both junior and senior to yourself. It implies a dependence both on ideas, and on others. It is part of the essential administrative cement in a democratic society' (Lello, 1979, p. 10). These words, written in 1979 at the end of an introductory chapter to a collection of essays about accountability, are still a fair description of its meaning. This book analyses the practice of accountability which has now become the hallmark of the government's policies in education. It is intended for a wide variety of people who are bound up with the current innovations for which they are answerable or by which they are directly affected.

Parents now have much more power within the school and especially within the governing body but it is a power for which they are answerable to other parents, to the staff, and to the government; they are principally answerable to the children, and as parents their accountability to them will be shown in the fulfilment and vocational success of their offspring in later life. It is not only essential that they should understand what is happening around them in education; it is unavoidable.

Teachers only see a part of the story, although they understand it clearly because they are actually putting the ideas into practice. In teaching the curriculum they are at the sharp end. Without a detailed awareness of what they are doing in the classroom it would be quite impossible for them to do their job. In this respect they fully understand what it means to be accountable. What they do not always see so readily is how the practice of accountability applies in other parts of the educational system. It would be unfortunate if they could not see their place in the wider framework; if they could, it would enhance their effectiveness in their more specific role.

Administrators rarely see the wider picture, but they are always affected by it and usually have to pretend to know it. They have a difficult task to undertake: their role is to implement national or local government decisions, and yet they try to do more. They always seek to insert an input of their own and it is important for them to do so, because their work is often so humdrum and boring. But their own contributions always have to be within the guidelines set by their political masters. This is hard for some of them but it helps if they understand the general framework within which they work.

Politicians, both local and national, usually have direct contact with each other and it works best if one is not subservient to the other. The wider view of accountability is valuable for all of them, and they realize that when they see the complete picture they can more easily interpret it in their own political situation.

It is already clear that there are different sorts of accountability: what is intrinsic to the work of the teacher is not always intrinsic to the work of the politician. The key question is whether these different sorts of accountability are in the same category. Is the financial accountability of a governing body comparable to the moral accountability of a teacher? Is the accountability of a parent in a school the same as the accountability of the local MP? The answer is that all of these people are dealing with the same subject but approaching it from different angles. Clearly they are all answerable in one way or another but although they are not answerable in the same way they are all called to give an account, or to explain their actions. It is this act of being 'put on the spot', of having 'to stand up and be counted', or of 'defending a corner' which they have in common and which links everybody in education. This is the administrative cement mentioned in the opening paragraph.

It was Prime Minister James Callaghan who started the public debate about accountability in education, in a speech at Ruskin College in October 1976:

Public interest is strong and will be satisfied. It is legitimate. We spend £6 billion on education so there will be discussion. If everything is reduced to such phrases as 'educational freedom versus state control' we shall get nowhere. . . . Where there is legitimate public concern it will be to the advantage of all involved in the educational field if these concerns are aired and shortcomings or fears put to rest.

It was no jump at all from this speech to growth in public concern about public accountability. For many, this took the form of an investigation into the most expensive part of the education service – the teaching profession – and the expression of this as the serious consideration, and often introduction, of teacher appraisal. Montgomery and Hadfield in *Practical Teacher Appraisal* (1989) wrote, '. . . it is not unreasonable that the taxpayer should expect teachers and others to be accountable. The main issues are how, and to whom and in what form.' These comments are about as directly practical as it would be possible to get and the whole issue has always been at the level of what the government is doing rather than about the philosophical implications of the word. Whitfield, in *Curriculum Planning, Teaching and Education Accountability* (1976) introduces a moral imperative: 'Anyone who uses resources provided by others is in a position of stewardship, and accountability places two obligations upon the steward. Firstly a statement must be rendered and secondly there must be an examination of that statement.' Whitfield is insisting that information and explanation are intrinsic to accountability and that they are the anticipated voluntary actions of the steward. They are things that ought to be done; the moral obligation is unavoidable.

Since then the situation has changed, partly because the structure of education is laced with a variety of strategies which self-consciously seek to construct a fully accountable system. Wagner in *Accountability in Education* (1989) quotes Arthur Rice in *The Nation's Schools* (US, 1970). 'Public education is not our special birthright. Rather it is a tax supported service in which teachers participate. Public education belongs to all the people, and all the people have the right to seek its improvement, to determine its purposes, and to evaluate its outcomes.' Wagner believes this is an unmanageable concept because it implies more cohesion within the people than could actually exist and also because there are various conceptions of accountability which would have to be separated from each other before common goals can be agreed. I believe he is completely wrong about this, and the development of patterns of accountability in Britain during the last five years demonstrates it.

To begin with, the amount of power which has been given to people in schools, and which they have effectively accepted, has been quite enormous. It is real power which deals with money and the appointment of staff, and it includes the provision of lay inspectors with powers of inspection in schools. Secondly, those involved have shown considerable cohesion and have united in parents' meetings at which school reports have been presented by the head and other important school figures. Parents have a majority on governing bodies and many such bodies are led by them. Wagner's mistake is to construct a philosophical category in an area which should be mainly practical. This is why the present book is needed, which seeks to look at the practical working of accountability.

The increase in the power of parents has led, and is leading, to some radical rethinking of many aspects of education. One is the wish on the part of many parents to reintroduce streaming, 'where it had been forgotten, ignored, or deliberately avoided and even shunned'. This quotation is from the Parental and Schools Choice Interaction study, led by Phil Woods, which monitors changes in schools and is undertaken by the Open University with funding from the Economic and Social Research Council and was reported in the *Daily Mail* on 29 March 1992. It is the kind of controversy which has already started to cause comment, and will continue to do so.

The demand has come not only from parents but also from the government, because although a return to the 11-plus is not envisaged it is hoped that streaming can be reintroduced, thus increasing the choice open to parents. The teachers' unions are divided. The NUT (National Union of Teachers) considers streaming a rigid dictatorial system but the National Association of Schoolmasters/Union of Women Teachers (NAS/UWT) thinks it is often a good idea provided that no one dictates to the schools which teaching system is best for them. Roy Hattersley, writing in the *Sunday Times* on 3 January 1993, entitled his article 'Second-rate schooling, here we come' – in this he was referring not to streaming within a school but to a system which lavishes 'praise and resources on a few favoured establishments, and shame[s] and shock[s] the rest into emulating their achievements'. This would create a level of competition he deplores. The Junior Education Minister, Eric Forth, accepted in December 1992 that limited selection represented 'another step away from the uniformity which has held back schools for so long'.

The point of chasing this example is to give an illustration of the significant change that is quietly being effected by parents. Mr Hattersley or Mr Forth may say what they like but it is the parents who in the end have the most telling power.

This book looks carefully at all the specific areas where accountability is being practised. One is in the creation of grant-maintained schools, which have been accorded great freedom. Another is the creation of City Technology Colleges (CTCs), described by the chief executive, Susan Fey, as 'a small network of exemplar schools with the independence and autonomy to work on research and development models of a particular kind of education'. Of even greater significance, however, has been the change in the nature of the head's work. In 1991 David Hart, of the National Association of Head Teachers (NAHT), stated that the responsibilities associated with delegated budgets, and the advent of governors with significantly enhanced powers, 'have placed the management of schools by head teachers under a degree of scrutiny unparalleled in the education service'. He continued: 'heads are far more accountable and under greater pressure than ever before'. These words succinctly indicate the change in the head's role. There have been comparable changes in the reduction in numbers and in the marginalization of Her Majesty's Inspectors (HMI).

It is perhaps in the transformation of the power and the authority of the local education authorities (LEAs) that the greatest reforms lie and where the tough implementation of the new principles of accountability can be seen. This is considered in detail in Chapter 3 but it is worth noting here that the decline in the power of the LEAs must be associated with the increased concentration of power in central government, and in particular in the Secretary of State for Education.

There are three considerations relating to the increased power given to the Secretary of State. The first is simply to ask if there are enough people of sufficient calibre to fill the post, since it is now such a significant one. The second is whether the increased bureaucracy required to service the much larger central administration is the most economic use of resources. The third is whether increased centralization can actually work; is this the most appropriate way of running the education of the country?

Accountability in Practice is an attempt to describe the situation as it really is, not to make a theoretical construct. Much of the book is about what is happening. It does not seek to be critical, although in some parts this has seemed necessary. It is not written from a particular political point of view, but some comments do express an opinion which can be so interpreted. This is unavoidable, because so much of the legislation during the last five years has been overtly political; even to describe what has happened has often felt like writing a political pamphlet. This is more of a record than a guidebook. For example, it would not be possible to discover within these pages what a governing body should do if it wishes to opt out, but it would be helpful to read the appropriate section before beginning the process, in order to understand how it all fits in with government policy. Indeed, fitting in with government policy might be the subtitle of the book.

Chapter 2

Central Government

SECRETARY OF STATE FOR EDUCATION

This senior government cabinet post, established in 1964, constituted a change in the title and function of the office of Minister of Education, which had been created in 1944 and had arisen out of the position of President of the Board of Education. The 1944 Education Act stated that the Minister should

> promote the education of the people of England and Wales and the progressive development of institutions devoted to that purpose, and to secure the effective execution by local authorities, under his control and direction, of the national policy for providing a varied and comprehensive educational service in every area.

In 1944 there had been serious doubts about whether the Minister should have such power but the President of the Board was quite clear that his successor should have enough authority to compel backward authorities to raise their standards.

The Secretary of State has no less power nowadays, although his terms of reference have been modified. They can be summarized as follows. He is accountable to parliament for the direction and control of the education system, must represent education in the cabinet, and compete with other departments for money. He should establish new policies and directions for the education system, work within the statutory obligations of legislation, and seek to represent government policy. He should represent the DES in the national media. He should seek the views of, and listen to, national organizations, and the education lobby. He should agree with or veto local authority proposals.

Is it a strong position? A leader in the *Guardian* in July 1986 commented on this whole question:

> The Secretary of State for Education and Science is by no means as powerful a minister as he appears to be. He proposes, but the education authorities dispose. He can set up enquiries, he can wheedle money out of the Treasury, he can make as many elegant speeches as he has time to compose. But he has relatively little control over the way that the authorities, much less the teachers themselves, actually behave.

It is unthinkable that such a passage could be written today. To begin with, the duties and responsibilities of local education authorities have been seriously pruned, and they are facing extinction; their condition is terminal. It has also become very clear that the Secretary of State has considerable power and effect on the LEAs; there is no question now of the LEAs' disposing unacceptably what the Secretary has proposed. The way in which teachers themselves have been persuaded or dissuaded from striking, or taking any disruptive union action, has also demonstrated that the Secretary of State's position in the cabinet gives him considerable strength; when the government discusses union militancy in general terms, the legislation applies to teachers who choose to take action as well as to any other citizen. In short, the latest wholesale transformation of the education system has been the work of all the cabinet even if the detailed work and the lion's share of the responsibility has, correctly, been shouldered by the Department for Education (DfE). In this way, the Secretary of State for Education is an even more powerful person than he appears.

THE EDUCATION REFORM ACT 1988

This major Act is a critical instrument of accountability and will be considered under five headings: curriculum; finance; grant-maintained schools and City Technology Colleges; charges for optional extras; and higher education.

Curriculum

The 1988 Act states that 'The curriculum must be balanced and broad and must promote the spiritual, moral, cultural, mental and physical development of pupils at the school and in society, and prepare pupils for the opportunities, responsibilities and experiences of adult life.' There is a basic curriculum called 'the National Curriculum', which consists of three main parts: the core subjects – maths, English, religious education, science (and Welsh in Welsh-speaking schools) – the foundation subjects – history, geography, technology, music, art, physical education, modern foreign languages (including Welsh in non-Welsh-speaking schools) – and cross-curricular themes like European awareness. Accountability is provided by the creation of attainment targets at each stage of the process. There are four Key Stages and the tests come at the end of each stage, at the ages of 7, 11, 14 and 16. At the same time all children follow prescribed programmes of study which correspond with each Key Stage and involve pupils taking examinations. So at each stage the child is being checked and monitored. To whom is the child accountable as a result of this curriculum organization?

He or she is clearly answerable to the teacher, the parents and the peer group. But what of himself? This last recognition is the most telling of all. The Act says nothing about the child's accountability to himself but there will be no young person for whom this regular testing will not become a personal challenge. The market-place has come not only into the organization of the school but also into the individual conscience of the child.

The Act also contains special sections about religious worship and religious education. The first makes it clear that worship 'must be wholly or mainly of a broadly Christian character though not distinctive of any Christian denomination'; nothing could more clearly relate the Act to traditional Christianity. It does not matter whether this was paying lip service to the dying vestiges of a religion or the necessary acknowledgement of a vibrant influence; the essential point of this section is that the Act is the expression of a moral or spiritual accountability, whether justifiable or not.

The more formal recognition of accountability came from the creation of the National Curriculum Council (NCC) and the School Examinations and Assessment Council (SEAC), now merged, both of which are answerable to the Secretary of State. They publish regular reports on the curriculum, and the research and investigations associated with it.

Finance

> LEAs have a duty to prepare and submit to the Secretary of State schemes to determine the distribution of expenditure between all county and voluntary schools they maintain and for delegating to the relevant governing bodies the responsibility for managing their share.
>
> LEAs have the duty to give the governing bodies of qualifying schools the responsibility for the school's budget share for the year.
>
> Within the constraints of the scheme the governing body can spend the budget as they think fit for the purpose of running the school and they can, if they wish, and if the scheme so permits, delegate the power to the Head.

These three critical extracts from the Act indicate the ways in which financial accountability is to be managed. LEAs are to calculate a formula for each school based on several key factors such as the total number of children in the school, the size and nature of the plant, and so on. On the basis of this formula the financial allocation for the school will be calculated. The school governors must then work out how the budget will be spent in relation to all the different demands upon it, not the least of which is staff salaries. The LEA must also work out the most productive ways of organizing and legislating for the remainder of its financial obligations; one of the most radical innovations has been the introduction of competitive tendering for cleaning, catering, ground maintenance, and the repair and maintenance of vehicles. What it amounts to is that maintained schools are now running themselves. LEAs are working much more in the financial market-place. Both schools and authorities are accountable to a variety of people, but accountable they surely are. The financial provisions of the 1988 Act, while giving a surprising amount of freedom to schools, also make heavy demands upon their capacity to account for and monitor what they spend. Freedom has entailed more work.

One of the important implications has been the way in which the balance of staff of a school would be determined. Put at the simplest level, would it be better to appoint a 50-year-old with experience but at considerable expense or to enrol two probationer teachers for the same price? Questions about staffing are usually much more complicated than this, but this example makes the point that the governors of a school are expressing a form of accountability to themselves because they have to live with the decisions they take.

Grant-maintained schools and City Technology Colleges

These two new school designations were brand-new additions to the educational scene.

Grant-maintained schools are those in which a majority of parents in a particular school choose to leave the LEA and put themselves under the direct control of the Department for Education. If a simple majority vote for this option they must agree not to change the character of the school; if it is a grammar school when it changes its status it must not change its character and become a comprehensive school. As a school it can receive property rights transferred from the LEA, acquire property, enter into contracts, invest money and accept and use gifts.

The real importance of these provisions is that they enable schools to escape the domination of the local authority if it becomes too dictatorial. Gone are the days when an LEA could browbeat or deviously outwit a hard-working but innocent head. If interference becomes too oppressive the parents are now permitted to remove themselves from the LEA's control, but it is only the parents who have this right and not the teachers or the governors, except those who are parents. Already this power is having a good effect upon education officers and politicians. City Technology Colleges are a serious attempt to raise the level of technological education. They must be situated in an urban area, provide for pupils of different abilities in the 11 to 18 range from the school's locality, and have a broad curriculum, with emphasis on science and technology.

Charges for optional extras

This minor and yet important clause simply allows charges to be raised from parents, provided the parents have agreed. It ends a considerable amount of illegality and makes possible a variety of plans which had previously been out of the question. Opponents of the scheme were clear that this would make the middle-class schools even better off than before and could leave schools in working-class areas even more impoverished; the truth could well turn out to be very different, for it has been assumed that schools in certain areas will have predictable futures. The results are likely to be different if the families are hard-working immigrants, if the governors of a school grasp the nettle of local responsibility and develop pride in the local school, if a locally based industry 'adopts' a school in the district, or in a host of other particular circumstances.

Higher education

The Act contains particular provisions which affect the funding of higher education. These are all discussed elsewhere, but will be repeated here for the sake of completeness. Some have already been superseded. The Polytechnics and Colleges Funding Council (PCFC), which replaced the National Advisory Body for Public Sector Higher Education, and the Universities Funding Council (UFC), which replaced the University Grants Committee (UGC), have been replaced by the Higher Education Funding Council (HEFC) which now serves both polytechnics and universities.

What caused greater consternation was the abolition of life-tenured appointments for all new academic appointments to universities. This, of course, raised more than purely financial issues. It removed at once the security of tenure which has been both the curse and the strength of many university appointments. The curse was the risk of complacency, which militated against good teaching and research; the strength was that tenure removed financial strain from the lecturer, who could concentrate on work.

Soon after the Act became law the Education Secretary sharpened his attitude towards university teachers and instituted a system by which their teaching performance was to be assessed every three years. Pat Partington, director of the Universities Staff Development and Training Unit, warned that the government's approach was too simplistic: 'If there are areas of neglect, then you need to help people to improve. The question is how you support staff, not one of moving into those areas in a punitive way.'

In all of the five areas of this 1988 Act which have been discussed in this chapter, the changes have been considerable. The curriculum revolution has been fully launched. The financial provisions have already been implemented. Grant-maintained schools and City Technology Colleges already exist and are still being founded. Charges for optional extras have been fully instituted. Higher education is in the throes of massive change. The Act has indeed become a critical instrument for change.

HER MAJESTY'S INSPECTORS (HMIs)

The Schools Act of 1992 revolutionized the arrangements for the inspection of schools. It had two main parts.

1. There will be established Chief Inspectors of Schools for England and Wales to advise the Secretary of State, to regulate new arrangements for school inspection by setting up a register of independent inspectors and to monitor and guide the activities of those registered to inspect. Each Chief Inspector will report annually to parliament from evidence gathered by the accredited inspection teams. This will cover the quality of education provided, the standards achieved, and the efficient management of financial resources.

2. Registered Inspectors will be put on a register after satisfactorily completing two stages in the training and preparation. The first is a residential week in which those wishing to be put on the list of registered inspectors will be introduced to the pattern which the Chief HMIs have devised for the inspection of schools; at the same time they will be assessed for their suitability. The second is to take part in a genuine school inspection and be assessed while this is taking place. After satisfactorily completing these two stages, the registered inspector will then be put on a list which will be circulated and available to all those educational institutions which OFSTED (Office for Standards in Education) will wish to be inspected. It will be the duty of the particular Authority to ensure that the school is inspected regularly. The inspecting teams will be led by a registered inspector and should include at least one member without personal experience of school management or education and whose primary function is not that of providing financial or business expertise.

When the register is circulated, the LEAs, or the governors in the case of the grant-maintained schools, will have to invite at least two tenders for their inspections. Prior to this, all the required information will have had to have been sent, the inspection takes place involving all aspects of the school including relations with and the part played by parents. The written report, a summary of it, and a plan of action for the future will be sent to the Chief Inspector, the LEA or the governing body, and be made available to members of the general public.

These were momentous proposals. The great army of HMIs had been drastically reduced. Gone was the power of LEAs reinforced by their own inspection programmes. Gone was the unwillingness to discuss education at certain levels. In had come total involvement of all parties, intense scrutiny by regular inspection, greater accountability in every aspect of education including by inspection, and the setting up of national guidelines for the work of registered inspectors. Most important of all was the permanent recognition that schools were more detached than they had been ten years ago and now had all the responsibilities and opportunities that independence brought, as well as the increased burdens. The sharp end to all this new freedom was that schools would be regularly inspected, monitored and checked.

Before the reforms were introduced, Eric Bolton, former senior chief inspector, and John Burchill, chief inspector for Wandsworth in London, thought that some form of new machinery for increasing accountability would have to be introduced although they were not clear about the form it should take. Vernon Bogdanor, Fellow of Brasenose College and Reader in Government at Oxford, writing in the *TES* (14 June 1991), believed that the reforms were part of a move to centralize the education service and that this would create serious problems: 'The purpose behind the centralisation of education is to make schools responsive to the market rather than to the political caprice of elected authorities.' Bogdanor thinks this will fail because

> it will be found to offend against fundamental democratic norms. Moreover, the policy is quite out of line with the direction in which our partners in the European Community are moving . . . that public services should be taken at the lowest level of government consistent with efficiency . . . the principle of subsidiarity.

In a letter in the *Independent* on 29 January 1992, signed by twenty-one representatives of leading educational organizations, unions and action groups, concern was expressed that the provision that schools should choose their own inspectors 'is wholly inconsistent' with the independence of those inspecting the schools and 'should be abandoned'. It continued: 'standards for schools should be consistently high across the country. It is essential that the inspectorate has a national perspective based on extensive contact with schools in order to advise the Government and inform the public.' One headline in the *Times Educational Supplement* (*TES*) asked: 'Will the New Army Pass Muster?'

It might be helpful to conclude this section on the central government by listing the five major agencies which impinge to a greater or lesser degree on education. First is the Department for Education, formerly the Department of Education and Science (DES), which is responsible for a national policy working through the LEA. The role of this department is not as clear as it was; some schools have opted out, some colleges are incorporated, the HMI has been largely privatized, and higher education is 'far off' and hot to handle.

Second is the Treasury, which determines the amount of money to be spent nationally. As always, allocation of funds involves working out and working through a list of the priorities of the government of the day. Education costs a lot of money and the way it is spent is determined in no small measure by the Treasury.

Third is the Audit Commission, a powerful agency which monitors the efficient spending of the financial allocations of the Treasury. To ignore the effect of the Audit Commission on education as on every other aspect of government is to ignore one of the most important unsung influences.

Fourth is the Manpower Services Commission, which has had a major responsibility for enhancing the provision of vocational education in schools and colleges for several years. It has encouraged new and innovative approaches including the Youth Training Scheme (YTS) and the Technical and Vocational Education Initiative (TVEI).

Fifth and sixth are the Department of the Environment and the Department of Employment; both are important, but less central than the previous bodies.

Ian Lawrence, in *Power and Politics at the Department of Education and Science*, argues that the 'origination of education policy will only flourish and be effectively managed by four relationship puzzles: between the DES and Parliament, within the DES between politicians and administrators, between central government and local government, teachers or lecturers and their employers'. The DES has now become the DfE, but the four-sided tension is still present. Whether it is creative or not is far from clear.

Chapter 3

Local Government

LOCAL EDUCATION AUTHORITIES

'We should not be looking at what a local authority can provide or control but at what the local community wants and how the authority can offer it to them', said Ossie Hopkins, the chief executive of Ribble Valley Borough Council and formerly deputy chief education officer in Birmingham. His words mirror the opinions of many district councils who are drawing up plans to take on the dwindling powers of education authorities. Dr Riley, the senior research officer with the Institute of Local Government Studies (Inlogov), did not foresee in August 1992 that this assumption of power would follow a standard pattern. 'It will depend on a number of factors including the number of opted out schools in the area. The norm will be that there won't be any norm.' (Riley, *TES*, August 1992). But the seeds of the radical changes are already sown and they are growing in the financial premises where LEAs have always worked. It has been assumed that the LEA was critically necessary as a middle tier between the national government and the schools. LEAs have always made this assumption and shouldered their power with responsibility and conscientiousness. Now, however, the balance is changing and the part that is disappearing is the LEA; this silent revolution is happening with minimal disturbance. Perhaps the characteristically unobtrusive exercise of local control is more difficult to defend because of its subtlety. 'Put the people first' was the simple solution of Howard Davies, controller of the Audit Commission. Bogdanor was less clear, when he asked in a *TES* article on 14 June 1991, 'Where will the buck stop?'

Power shifted with the creation of the National Curriculum Council, the Citizen's Charter, the School Examinations and Assessment Council, open enrolment, City Technology Colleges, grant-maintained schools and the introduction of local management of schools (LMS). None of these changes taken individually would have been so significant, but together they are a revolutionary set of reforms and a major assault on the traditional areas of local authority power. The LEAs had become unnecessary, expensive, and distracting to the main thrust of the government's educational policy.

It was hardly surprising that there was so little opposition to the quiet destruction of this wasteful middle tier. Moans from parents about 'the County' or 'the Authority' were time-honoured complaints which had customarily been shelved. The responses to any query usually followed a consistent pattern. Reduced to basics, any reply was bland, evasive, or high-handed. The power the administrators wielded to control a rebel or a 'troublemaker' was that he or she would stand no chance of another job unless they complied with the accepted code. There was little alternative for teachers but to join the HMI, yet admission to that august body was not easy and in some ways restricted. It might have seemed like jumping out of the frying pan and into the goldfish bowl.

But the real beginning of serious disenchantment with LEAs came with the reorganization of secondary education in the 1960s and 1970s. At the same time as parents were being told of the great virtues of having all children walk through the same door of the same comprehensive school, they were also being told that unless they agreed to the new proposals there would be no money for the un-reorganized school in the future. It was a bribe with smiles that left no room for genuine negotiation.

The introduction of comprehensive education was not really a party political issue, although it often masqueraded as such. It became an issue which the political left successfully manipulated to create a bandwagon of support with no serious emotional commitment. In the early days, before education had become a top issue, it was easy for Prime Minister Harold Wilson to say that 'grammar schools will only be abolished over my dead body', but it was a phrase he chose to forget as the socialist campaign within the country got under way and it became clear that there were those in his own party who saw the destruction of the existing educational structure as the most effective way of dismembering society and replacing it with their own plans. It was while Margaret Thatcher was at the DES and later when she became Prime Minister that the number of reorganized schools significantly increased. The electorate may have been divided on party lines but the political parties themselves showed no evidence of such division in policies or actions. This difference between personal belief and published party programme caused distrust from all except the unswerving ideologues who were determined to strike at the heart of national stability through their deep educational proposals. It is this difference, rooted in the conviction that LEAs must do what the majority vote for, which has led, in part, to the demand for greater accountability of LEAs.

The issue was, however, much more ideas than money, because voters clearly want more control over the education of their children. Ideologues who want to advance Marxist philosophy are still allowed to distribute leaflets in the market-place but will only have their ideas supported in the Education Committee if the majority of voters both understand the proposals and then are prepared to vote for them. The organization and the reorganization of secondary education provided the context from which sprang the vigorous comprehensives needing accountability. The present Conservative government has responded to this groundswell of demand by involving parents in school governing bodies, giving greater control over spending in schools, and allowing schools to opt out of control by the LEA, the middle tier.

Everywhere during Margaret Thatcher's years as Prime Minister the country was being exposed to competition and open management. It was unthinkable that education should remain unaffected while everything else was in a state of flux, because education does not have an existence separate from the context within which it works. It always depends upon constituents in society such as economic recession, or employment, or parental attitudes. If the whole national scene was changing it was only a matter of time before education would also be affected. Even the City was assaulted: status and educational pedigree were being replaced by the ability to 'do the job'. This usually meant achieving certain objectives and making things work. The 'Big Bang' did not wear an old school tie; nor did the grocer's daughter from Grantham. There were times when these changes sounded remarkably like socialism but to avoid using this word the changes were called radical and this avoided misunderstanding and confusion. The end product was that local education authorities came under scrutiny, like everything else. Accountability had reached County Hall.

In one authority, the East Sussex Accountability Project (1982) saw accountability as not 'so much a programme, more a way of life' and believed that the whole of education would be subject to its rigours. By 1988 Sheila Lawlor, in her explosive pamphlet *Away with LEA's*, written for the Centre for Policy Studies, saw LEAs of the future as 'merely acting as funding agencies and brokers'. She continued:

> the powers and responsibilities of LEAs as they now exist must, therefore, be reduced so that it is to the teacher that the initiative in teaching falls; that it is to the head that the initiative in running his school devolves; and that choice of school for parents becomes a reality: not a choice of uniform mediocrity but a choice of what is best to educate the diverse talents of their children.

A thorough and more analytical report, prepared by the consultants Coopers & Lybrand for the DES, was presented in 1988. This deals with the local management of schools and does not restrict the terms of reference of the investigation to the purely financial: 'The changes require a new culture and philosophy of the organisation of education at the school level. They are more than purely financial; they need a general shift in management.' The underlying philosophy of financial delegation stems from the application of the principles of good management which start with the identification of objectives and move on to the measurement of how they are to be attained. The authors saw that there would be major gains from such delegation:

> It will increase the accountability of schools for providing value for money; it will give schools the flexibility to respond directly and promptly to the needs of the school and its pupils in a way which will increase the effectiveness and quality of the services provided. Schools will have more incentive to seek efficiency and economy in their use of their resources.

But they saw LMS as being even more concerned with effectiveness than with efficiency: 'it is more concerned with the "value" component in value-for-money rather than with the "money" component'.

Other advantages were also expected. LEAs would see more clearly what they required from schools; schools would understand better the pressures on the LEAs. A headteacher's job would 'be more complete and satisfying'. LMS would also give a school the chance to change or not to change a whole range of policies. But much of the success would depend upon the attitudes of the schools and the staff within them and it would be essential that all the changes should be viewed from a positive point of view.

The effect of LMS upon the LEAs was that they lost detailed control of most school activities; that loss of control has also meant the loss of the considerable power which went with it: the power to delay, to implement, and the power to encourage those ideas with which the authority was in sympathy as well as those it preferred to shelve.

LEAs chose to implement their ideas on the basis of a 'resource allocation formula'. This was a method of determining which responsibilities would remain with the LEA and which should be taken over by the school. There are three components in this formula. One is based on pupil numbers, with suitable adjustments where necessary. Secondly there is a flat rate for each school linked to the particular need of some sites. Thirdly there is a component for special activities, for example the use of the school by the community. The local education authority continues to have responsibility for some parts of the education and support services in the area, but its role in the management of schools is considerably reduced.

In 1989 the Audit Commission in a paper, 'Losing an empire – finding a role: the LEA of the future', proposed six roles for the reduced authority, as:

(1) a leader, articulating a vision of what the education service is trying to achieve;

(2) a partner, supporting schools and colleges and helping them to fulfil this vision;

(3) a planner of future facilities with the responsibility to rationalize surplus capacity – a job not well done in the past;

(4) a provider of information, helping people to make informed choices;

(5) a regulator of quality, based on a more structured approach to inspection;

(6)   a bank manager, channelling funds which allow local institutions to deliver.

In the *TES* of 2 August 1991, Howard Davies, controller of the Audit Commission, in an article entitled 'Put the people first', reviewed the situation in relation to the reforms and concluded that the government's attitude to the authorities had hardened. Grant-maintained schools were becoming a more significant feature on the educational landscape. Many authorities had not slimmed down their budgets sufficiently and their unwillingness to 'grasp the nettle' had been highlighted by the publication of league tables (Section 42). Much provision for 16-to-18-year-olds had been removed from authority control, a fact not unrelated to the abolition of the Community Charge. There has been a major review of the inspectorate of which local inspectors are a part. 'All of this comes together in what I see as a government view that authorities are, for the most part, an encumbrance to the reform agenda rather than a means of achieving it.'

These strident words of Howard Davies strike at the heart of any future for local education authorities. Indeed there is already a gradual crumbling of LEA services, a continued unwillingness on the part of some authorities to recognize that the balance of power has shifted, and a hope that a change of power in central government will enable LEAs to return to their old patterns. There is every indication that other political parties would be only too willing to continue the massive pruning which the Conservative government has already undertaken; they might not go for the same solutions, but nor would they return to the old situation where the LEA had almost sovereign power in some areas. Jack Straw, then Shadow Secretary of Education, wrote in the *Education Times* of 21 October 1991 of a rigorous relationship between the authorities and the schools: 'What we want to see is schools' effectiveness measured – or to use a fashionable market analogy, the "education value added" which a school creates'.

In November 1991, Area One of the Secondary Heads Association in London distributed a discussion document listing the services that should be supplied by an intermediate body between school and government. It is by no means definitive, nor is it meant to be, but it does provide a useful checklist, so is worth including here. It does leave key questions remaining and only time will reveal the answers, because so many of the reforms over the last five years have not been fully digested or made fully operational; whatever the eventual outcome the essential principles are that education should be a service, that some middle tier is required, that the system should be planned and coherent, and that maximum freedom should be delegated to school level.

A. Services that such a body *must* provide:

FINANCE	– Audit
	– GEST (Grants for Education Support and Training) administration
	– Oversight of contracts
	– Set local budgets
PLANNING	– Admissions
	– Consultation procedures
	– Information service
PARENT SUPPORT	– Complaints procedures
	– Information service
PUPIL SUPPORT	– Attendance
	– Awards for higher education, etc.
	– Special educational needs
	– Transport
	– Welfare benefits
QUALITY ASSURANCE	

B. Services that we would *like* to be provided:

PUPIL SUPPORT	– Careers Service
	– Curriculum support centres (libraries/museums/study centres, etc.)
	– Extra-curricular music/drama/sport
	– Work experience
SCHOOL SUPPORT	– Economic purchasing arrangements
	– Dissemination of good practice
	– Legal advice
	– Personnel services

- Promoting local schools and achievements
- Staffing (recruitment/retention/ relocation expenses/combating teacher shortage)

C. Services that we would like provided by *an agency into which we could buy*:

MANAGEMENT
SUPPORT FOR
- Energy
- Finances
- Property

SUPPORT SERVICES
- Area administration
- Building services
- Cleaning and caretaking
- Curriculum
- Education welfare
- Exchequer (payroll, pensions, etc.)
- Grounds maintenance
- Information technology
- School Psychological Service

TRAINING
- Staff
- Governors
- Financial management
- Inset
- Probationers' support
- Professional support

LOCAL MANAGEMENT OF SCHOOLS

Reduced to the simplest meaning, this initiative shifts lost power to schools and makes it impossible for local education authorities to manage schools in the future as they have done in the past. It is an immense change.

One of the principal changes in the Education Act 1988 was that there should be greater delegation of financial responsibility and other forms of management from the LEA to the schools. The government commissioned Coopers and Lybrand to consider this aspect of the Act and their report was largely adopted without alteration.

The consultants concluded that the vast proportion of resources could be so delegated. They felt they had to consider a resource allocation formula even though this had not been within their remit and decided that it should contain three components. The first would be pupil number driven, which simply means that the financing would be based upon the numbers in the school; the second would be a flat rate different for each school and based upon the premises; the third would be related to special activities such as community involvement and the like. All this would remove the detailed running from the LEA's purview but would leave it in control of major policy issues.

This would, it was seen, mean a major change in the attitude of the schools themselves towards their responsibilities:

> LMS will succeed only if there is a positive attitude to it from the head, the staff, and the governing body. It will require a recognition that it is school management that is required, not simply an increase in administration.

The consultants wrote in terms that were very refreshing to read in education circles: 'LMS is designed to enable schools to be more responsive, schools will need to devote thought to re-defining what it is they are seeking to respond to.' Or later in the report: 'we are under no illusions that many LEAs will find the process difficult and perhaps even unsettling. The tasks are not easy, nor are some of the decisions which will be needed. But the result, if done well, will help produce a more responsive and effective school system.'

Tim Brighouse, in the *TES* on 23 June 1989, perceived several of the major problems and time has proved him correct. He wrote that it was safer for LEAs to work hard at getting the details of LMS and all the other parts of the legislation right, 'so that they can support principles of interdependence and social justice and reflect a sensitive understanding of their communities' needs', and that means 'sharing information, supporting schools and teachers'. The truth is that officers in most LEAs have largely followed this line, but the elected members have often been less wise; in many cases they have been only too anxious to make political capital out of the situation. One of the unfortunate results of this irresponsible policy has been that schools have sometimes opted out because they resented interference. The authorities, elected members or not, do not seem to have realized that schools which are harassed now have the perfect answer to unacceptable treatment.

The extent of this revolutionary change has still to be fully appreciated and becomes more involved the more the complications unfold. There are major implications for staffing, the maintenance of buildings, and even such basic questions as the advisability of cheque-book management. Sometimes it has provoked confusion upon confusion about trivia, often because in a profession concerned with detail it is difficult to see any other way. Teachers do not perceive the grand strategy; it has not been in their experience. It therefore seems important to repeat the two objectives of LMS:

(1) to enable governing bodies and heads to plan their use to maximum effect in accordance with their own needs and priorities;
(2) to make schools more responsive to their clients – parents, pupils, the local community and employers.

Who would have expected such realistic objectives ten or even five years ago? But the practical results have often been very different from the legislative theory. Much of the pattern of the 1988 Act in relation to local management in schools was based on experience gained from the pilot experiment in Cambridgeshire, which had been started ten years earlier. The problems faced then had, by 1988, become more advanced and sophisticated. Peter Downes, head of Hichingbrooke School in Huntingdon, writing in the *TES* on 18 October 1991, tells of the serious effects of drastic cuts in the education budget with which he had to cope.

> We have installed our water-saving boys' urinal flushers, the electric hand driers, the more cost-effective telephone systems; we have negotiated better deals on our energy consumption tariffs and on our reprographics equipment; we have chased waste to the point where our colleagues wonder if an educational thought ever crosses our finance-numbed brains. There really is not much else left to reduce: the administrative demands of local management of schools, records of achievement and the national curriculum have increased the need for support staff; a minimal level of maintenance is unavoidable; we can scarcely risk imprisonment for refusing to pay the rates; we have not been able to spend anything on extra incentive allowances or discretionary payments so there's nothing to claw back in that area.

This description emphasizes how highly specific LMS has become. The head later reaches an important conclusion: 'The effect of LMS has been to bring educational finance out of dusty offices and into the limelight. Within a school, the budget, drafted by the head and/or deputy with help from a resource-management team, is subjected to rigorous scrutiny by the staff and governors. All the departmental allocations and incentive allowances are known and every heading of expenditure is challenged and justified.' Peter Downes ends with a telling paragraph:

> By introducing LMS, the Government has opened the door of the secret garden of education finance. It can never be shut again. Heads of governors, who now have the unenviable task of implementing difficult financial decisions imposed on them from afar, ought, I believe, to mount a campaign for access to central government financial information in a comprehensible format.

Local management of schools has wider effects than the purely financial. Governors and staff, especially heads, are now receiving an extended form of in-service training in areas with which they had previously been unfamiliar. They are meeting in groups to discuss real issues such as how to afford the cost of a senior member of staff by contrast with appointing a much cheaper person straight from college; sometimes the difference in cost is so significant that it amounts to saving the cost of half a teacher. From the point of view of the more mature teacher this can often spell doom unless that person has particular skills to offer. But it is not only in matters of staffing that there are new challenges. The costing of new materials or books is now the task of heads of departments, and indeed every member of a department; previously it was of only marginal significance and often meant no more than a grumble. This careful analysis of education from a financial angle means that all areas in the school benefit from the same tight management. The days when a discussion about the curriculum could be just a form of gentle relaxation have gone, and such matters are now treated with a seriousness which comes from the change in the total climate of the school. The style of the discussions of financial matters has greatly influenced the style in which all other matters are considered.

The effect on the LEAs has been deep and disturbing to them and their previous working methods, and although this will be discussed again later it is worth saying now that the influence of any organization usually depends upon controlling the financial side of the operation. When this disappears much real authority goes with it and the organization loses effective power because it loses the ultimate sanction. It is no longer true that a head can be 'brought to heel' by the withholding of money for a project, or by making it so ponderous to obtain that momentum goes out of the venture. The steam for this revolution in attitude has built up in the last five years. It represents a degree of liberation which transcends the formal administrative reforms. It is a major revolution.

As a result, the organization of local education authorities has undergone major restructuring because the old design was unsuitable for an organization which was already requiring regular financial monitoring by central government. Posts like 'education finance manager' were created so that the authority should know precisely what was going on financially. The overall effect was to rethink much of the organization which had previously been taken for granted but which with the new role of the authority needed reform or abolition. However, much of the work of the LEAs was to help schools prepare for what has become a very different method of working and consequently much effort was put into training courses run and arranged by a team on hand to give regular advice and guidance. It has also been customary for the changes to be standardized across schools and for them to be regularly monitored to ensure that all schools benefit from the best practices.

Parents seem to have welcomed greater participation in the running of schools. The whole composition of governing bodies has changed significantly, and it is this that must now be considered.

GOVERNORS

The jobs the governors are expected to do are various. They should determine the aims and policy of the school. They should allocate the school budget so that national requirements and individual pupils' needs are met. They should help interview and appoint staff. They should decide how the school is to be used outside school hours. They should foster good relations with parents and the local community. They should visit and get to know the school, attend governors' meetings, and give parents information.

All are volunteers and can be parents, teachers in the school, LEA governors, co-opted governors, foundation governors, and headteachers who have the choice whether or not to be governors of their own schools. Whatever their designation, the aim is that the composition of governing bodies should reflect the local communities.

Central government and local authorities provide resources, advice and training. Diocesan boards also support voluntary school governors. There are organizations such as Action for Governors' Information and Training (AGIT), the Institute of School and College Governors (ISCG), and the National Association of Governors and Managers (NAGM), which seek to represent the governors' point of view.

Stuart Maclure, former editor of the *TES*, wrote a column headed 'Beware the Power of Governors', realizing that their power potential was enormous. He asks the question: what are the limits of the powers of school governors? He answers this by stating that 'the law is not clear', and deepens the query by adding that, 'the head's responsibilities *vis-à-vis* the governors are undoubtedly vague'. He cites the example of the turmoil in an opted-out school in Stratford East and might have added the case of the suspended head of the Woodruffe School in Lyme Regis, in Dorset. Clearly he fears that there may be too much interference with heads, and quotes the Taunton Commission of 1868: 'our greatest headmasters have been those who have been least interfered with'.

The amount of exposure of all educational issues has been much greater than ever before. However, there is a disproportionate dearth of comparable publicity about the role of governors in the new educational designs. Their power is dominant, next only to the Secretary of State, and their position defined by Act of Parliament. They are unassailable. They are the rulers of the educational scene in any sense that matters. Their control over the financial running of the school is absolute and, provided they do not become profligate or criminal, it is secure. They can appoint, suspend and dismiss staff. They spend as long, and probably longer, discussing the ways in which the school should be run than the teachers. They come from all walks of life and from both sexes. They represent all ages. Parents are in a majority in any governing body. And yet their great authority receives less media coverage than any other aspect of educational life and controversy. It is not a secret power but it is one which has so far been neither perceived nor appreciated. These are early days, and there are already signs that those with this newly acquired power are beginning to flex their muscles.

The governors' ultimate weapon, and such it is, is that they can cause a school to opt out of LEA control and achieve grant-maintained status if they are dissatisfied with the way the school is being run from County Hall. If they don't like it they can leave, and all the ideologues in the world cannot stop such a move to state rather than local control from taking place. It is true that this major decision for any school or college needs a majority of the parents to support the idea, but in the past the leadership of the move has always come from the governing body, where parents form a majority. It is thus the responsible use of power by a democratically elected committee; it has effectively emasculated local education authorities, and they know it.

It was local management of schools which transformed the role of governors and sought to ensure the maximum delegation of financial and managerial responsibilities to governing bodies. The role of the governors, including the head, is to set objectives, construct a plan and arrange the resources designed to achieve it, and to report back regularly to the parents and the community. The overall result of this major change has varied considerably throughout the country, according to the annual report of the Chief HMI, Terry Melia, in 1992. Apparently it was difficult to recruit governors in many inner city areas, and in other places too much has been left to the head. Nevertheless, there had by contrast been a general improvement in effectiveness and 'some outstanding examples of governors acting in partnership with schools to construct and implement school development plans'. It was also noted that there had generally been a disappointing attendance at annual governors' meetings, which are now a statutory duty; in some schools no parents came at all.

There is a growing groundswell of discontent with the ways in which many LEAs have been niggardly about handing over graciously and correctly those time-honoured tasks which are being removed from their control. Many feel that items to which governing bodies are now entitled should be carefully enumerated and explained in the form of a contract. Many schools are grouping together to form consortia as a means of ensuring that the 'cake' is not only made available but is shared out equally. In short, as Nigel Gann, an educational consultant and a school governor, wrote in the *TES* in 1992, 'governors should tell councils what they expect from them'.

It is clear that by 1990 an increasingly large number of governors were being trained. This was a new idea, and was being masterminded by administrators who had never been governors themselves; even when the authority did include governors it was usually those people who would 'toe the party line'. Having a course for governors compartmentalized the functions of a school. There would be a course for deputy heads, one for heads, one for probationers, one for careers teachers, and now one for governors. There could be no argument against preparing people for new tasks. The result of these training courses, where they took place in any purposeful way, has been that a new breed of governors is being created who are better informed and could not so easily be hoodwinked. It also means that those who have been so prepared are expected to spend more time on the running of the school. There is much more work to do, because the objective of the whole exercise is to make parents more committed to the education of their children. Putting in a lot of time in meetings is the price that has to be paid for knowing how your child is being educated. If the courses are meant to solve problems they have failed, because they usually cause more to be revealed; an informed governing body is more likely to investigate the deeper implications of running a school than an ignorant one.

The kind of governor of yesteryear who turned up irregularly but was a major force in the town and a good public relations man in the market-place no longer has a part to play on the governing body. The reasons for this are clear, but the long-term loss in terms of goodwill is considerable. Now governors are becoming professional.

Chapter 4

Higher Education

'New centres of excellence' read the headline in the *Independent* on 25 February 1992. The article went on to applaud the expansion in the number of students attending universities. The process had really begun in 1963 with the Robbins Report, which stated that courses of higher education should be available for all those qualified by ability and attainment who wished to pursue them. The Major Government in 1991 sought a major overhaul of the whole of education including the tertiary sector and made it clear that the target was that 30 per cent of school-leavers should go on to higher education by the end of the century. The present view of higher education is wider than that of the Robbins committee, but the relentless expansionist drive was to continue.

The key statement of policy was issued by the government in May 1991: *Higher Education. A New Framework*. The distinction between universities and polytechnics was to be removed and there was to be a single framework for higher education, with seven main features:

(1) a single funding structure for universities, polytechnics and colleges of education;
(2) higher education funding councils within England, Scotland and Wales to distribute public funds for both teaching and research; and new links to continue the present close relationship with Northern Ireland's existing unitary structure;
(3) the extension of degree-awarding powers to major institutions

and the winding up of the Council for National Academic Awards (CNAA);

(4) extension of the title of university to those polytechnics which wished to use it and, subject to the development of suitable criteria, to other major institutions;

(5) external scrutiny of the quality control arrangements of UK higher education institutions by a UK-wide quality audit unit developed essentially by the institutions themselves;

(6) quality assessment units within each council to advise on relative quality across the institutions;

(7) co-operation between the councils to maintain a common approach to quality assessment.

This statement, together with the Education Reform Act 1988, forms the basis for much of the future shape of higher education. The third main influence is the decline in the number of school-leavers. Because the previous similar demographic change of the 1930s was less precisely measured, the possible effects of this one can only be speculated about. It may not actually mean fewer students but it may mean that to keep numbers of students up to the level the government seeks it will be necessary to offer incentives of some kind, maybe financial. It seems fair to assume that the demand for those with a higher education will continue to increase. The financing of this could be the weakness which prevents the expansion from taking place on the lines the government wishes.

UNIVERSITIES

Can the universities adapt themselves to a world of insecurity? Have they anything creative to contribute to it or are they themselves immersed, or about to be immersed, in the maelstrom? Can they 'rise to the height of the times'? All the familiar questions of university policy – questions of clientele, of curricula, of ways of living, of forms of government, of relations with the outside world – require to be rethought in the new perspective.

So wrote Walter Moberly, chairman of the University Committee in 1949, in his seminal book, *Crisis in the University* (p. 17). Over forty years later the same questions can still be put, with one significant difference: now it is necessary to include important sections on financial matters. In Moberly's book there is no mention of money.

Immediately after this passage Moberly quotes the celebrated Dr Hutchins, who had such a powerful effect upon American education at all levels in the 1930s and 1940s.

> Civilisation can be saved only by a moral, intellectual and spiritual revolution to match the scientific, technological and economic revolution in which we are now living. If education can contribute to a moral, intellectual and spiritual revolution, then it offers a real hope of salvation to suffering humanity everywhere. If it cannot, or will not contribute to this revolution, then it is irrelevant and its fate is immaterial.

It is the task of this section to explain the financial considerations which Moberly omitted, to assess their relevance, and to consider the current revolution at the tertiary level.

The University Grants Committee was established in 1919 and grew out of the Advisory Committee on University Grants. It was a difficult time for the universities. At the end of the war, student numbers were falling, endowments were no longer keeping pace with the rising cost of living, and local authority contributions had seriously declined. A conference in 1918 proposed the establishment of a standing committee to advise the government on financial provision for the universities, and the UGC was born.

The original terms of reference were 'to enquire into the financial needs of university education in the United Kingdom and to advise the government as to the application of any grants that may be made by Parliament towards meeting them'. The committee, of a chairman and eight members, was nominated by the Chancellor of the Exchequer. It reported to the Treasury, not to the president of the Board of Education because it was thought that the latter might interfere in academic matters. The Robbins Report of 1963 transferred responsibility to a reconstituted department under the Secretary of State for Education and Science.

Under this new arrangement only the chairman was full-time, with twenty members on the committee; fourteen were from universities and the rest from industry and other sectors of education. There was a permanent secretariat. In 1946 the terms of reference had changed to allow the UGC to take initiatives in the development of university education, which was how it was possible to accommodate the establishment of new universities in the 1960s. Of equal importance was the way in which the strictly financial functions of universities were administered by the UGC. It was aptly expressed in the annual report of the Committee of 1968-9:

> The Universities are independent, self-governing institutions, usually established by charter. They are free to conduct their own affairs and they are not subject to legislative control or ministerial directive. On the other hand, they depend on the state for the greater part of their funds; and they play an important part in the development of national policies and of the economy . . . In this situation, if the normal methods of control of government expenditure are not to be applied, there is a need for some intermediary between the state and the universities. There has to be some machinery which will enable public funds to flow into the universities without direct government intervention and which will reconcile the interests of the state as paymaster and the requirements of the universities; . . . there is a strong convention that the government does not enquire into or vary the advice.

In short, the UGC, an intermediate body, was given the task of distributing government funds, thus ensuring there was no direct government interference in university independence. Numerous sub-committees visited, discussed and reported back to the main body, but they were all within the UGC's control and direction.

The Education Act of 1992 changed these arrangements, because the government felt that universities were not sufficiently accountable for the very considerable sums of money they were receiving from the state. First the Act scrapped the binary system, enunciated by Anthony Crosland in his Woolwich speech of 1965 which stated that there should be two systems of higher education: the autonomous university system, and the other in the public sector consisting of the polytechnics, the colleges of education and the technical colleges. Two short-lived councils, the Universities Funding Council and the Polytechnics and Colleges Funding Council were combined in 1992 into the Higher Education Funding Council.

This controls the finances of polytechnics and universities in the newly merged higher education sector. The first chairman is Sir John Dearing, who has been chairman of both of the councils which the Higher Education Funding Council subsumed. The HEFC is part of government machinery and is not an intermediate body like the old UGC. Its powers are laid out in the Education

Act of 1988, and it provides advice to the Secretary of State on education and research in the universities.

'The Universities are bracing themselves for change,' commented Nicholas Pyke in November 1991 in the *TES*. The preceding White Paper had made it clear that universities would be made to accept public scrutiny of their standards. The article, headlined: 'Reform to trample hallowed ground', says that it is politically unacceptable for universities to be exempt from public scrutiny in a world where polytechnics have always been accountable. The latter have been answerable to the CNAA and the HMI but universities have had no comparable checks; even the appointment of external examiners often became a private deal with friends.

The object of the exercise is to see if universities can accept a larger number of students and at the same time continue to make financial savings. It is also hoped that greater accountability in the university sector will help it to see where savings can be made. Universities had expanded cheaply and quickly but this growth had been largely centred in the humanities and social sciences. Recently quality control has been investigated by the Academic Audit of the Committee of Vice-Chancellors and Principals of the Universities of the UK, who are visiting every university in the country, examining the monitoring procedures and making recommendations.

Quality assessment, which has received less attention, is the object of research by Gareth Williams at the London Institute of Education and Diana Green at Birmingham Polytechnic. Put bluntly, they are seeking to answer two questions: 'What is quality?' and 'How can it be measured?' These are not popular questions at any time, but now the universities are suspicious of any enquiry in case it leads to a cut in their grant or to the abolition of small, uneconomic departments. There is a fear that every government suggestion has a sinister ulterior motive. Even the principal opposition, the Labour Party, has suggested that it wishes to make 'the educational elite more answerable'. It has proposed the formation of a Higher Standards Council to monitor the merged polytechnic/university sector.

Mary Warnock in her pamphlet, *Universities: Knowing Our Minds* (1989) was highly critical of the proposed changes. She maintained that universities should be considered in different terms to those applied to schools. The universities must be seen as the source of new knowledge, the origin of that critical, undogmatic, imaginative examination of received wisdom without which a country cannot be expected to have its voice heard, and from which all intellectual standards flow. There is nowhere else that such intellectual authority can come from but the universities themselves. This is an area where the concept of the free market is simply not applicable. The universities may gradually influence the market; they cannot be subject to its immediate demands. (1989, p. 42)

Becher and Kogan, in *Calling Britain's Universities to Account* (1987) are equally critical of the changes being suggested. They write:

accountability and the working capacity of a relatively expensive system, far from being improved, will however be reduced and frustrated by the current policies of ministers and the small group of leading academics who seem anxious to join them in the march towards narrow selectivity and naively managerial ways of directing a sensitive and complex enterprise. . . . A government wishing to derive the maximum benefit from this field of endeavour must start from the democratic assumption that society needs an independent intelligentsia which is free from the close central prescription of its objectives. (1987, p. 3–4)

Peter Scott makes a telling point in *The Crisis of the University* (1984) when he claims that

the effective choice is really between different degrees and levels of accountability. So long as higher education receives the bulk of its income from public expenditure in direct and indirect forms, it cannot escape being accountable. . . . an earlier accountability to students, industry, and town hall was not replaced by an equally rigorous accountability to the state. This allowed a period of what A.H. Halsey has called 'donnish dominion' in which higher education was very much directed by the preoccupations of the academic profession. As a result the age of donnish dominion has drawn to a close to be replaced by a confused interregnum.

It is not as though all the answers can be found by raising money privately, not only because too many institutions are after the same crock of gold but because the old dichotomy between the respective values of the pure and the applied is being blurred. The relevance of much pure research is becoming obvious; Michael Elves of Glaxo makes it clear that spending on research in this pioneering chemical firm is by no means confined to that which gives a quick return. However, the best example comes from the department of organic chemistry at Manchester University where during an investigation into methods of synthesizing steroids the research team came across a substance which was later developed as the contraceptive pill. It is difficult for private concerns to know where best to invest for the future. There are even some surprises; the last Cambridge college to be built, Robinson, was financed by the profits from radio rentals. The Department of Archaeology at Cambridge University thrives on money from an engineer, Daniel McDonald, who endowed it with £10 million.

So there are confusions, whether the money is coming from some source of public funds, from bequests, endowments or donations, or from the range of university services, like conferences. The confusion really arises because the universities are changing their nature and to some extent their function as well. But they are also changing because the university must become accountable, whatever the source of the money. There is a general need for accountability to a whole range of people – government, governing bodies, employees, students, former students, other universities, donors and benefactors, the loan/creditor group and the public. They need to know about income and expenditure, and an explanation of the assets of the university. Without this information the likelihood of future financial support diminishes. It is not by chance that the Committee of Vice-Chancellors and Principals created an Accounting Standards Committee composed of representatives of all the professional institutes and associations involved with accountancy in Britain. Over several years the Committee has brought about a greater degree of uniformity in the preparation and presentation of university accounts and in 1989 they issued a Statement of Recommended Practice (SORP) to be followed by all universities. There may be confusion as to how money is obtained but there is no confusion as to how it is audited nor to whom the university is answerable for spending it.

This section began with a quotation from Moberly and it is appropriate to end with one: 'academic patriotism, however devoted and well-informed, does not exclude, but rather impels, a clear recognition and searching diagnosis of ailments'. It may not be clear that all the current ailments have yet been detected but the careful analysis of the role of the universities in the field of higher education, though painful, may well presage an invigorating reassessment of their place in society.

POLYTECHNICS

In June 1992 the Privy Council gave formal approval to the new university names of 28 polytechnics. Sheffield Poly became Sheffield Hallam University, a richly evocative and historical label, as was De Montfort University for Leicester; equally evocative was Liverpool John Moores University, the new name for Liverpool Polytechnic. Most commentators approved strongly of the new titles although Matthew d'Ancona, writing in *The Times* on 19 June 1992, commented that 'now, in the vast pool of universities, they may become unstuck, stripped of their distinctiveness, struggling always to be something else'. His article, 'Donnish delusions', claimed that name-changing is an amusing parlour game, but scarcely addresses the question: 'What makes a university?' D'Ancona quotes Cardinal Newman's *Idea of a University* (1873) and continues:

> polytechnics represent all that is modern, sleek and efficient, the universities have a mystique rooted in the dimly remembered past . . . Universities are expected by the nation to embody tradition, to flirt with church and state, to be oracular as well as expert. Such characteristics cannot be bolted on by legislation, however well-intentioned.

Time will tell, but many in the polytechnics rejoice that they now have style, dignity and title, and at least something approaching financial parity.

Polytechnics have often been forced to launch new ideas on small budgets. The Polytechnics and Colleges Funding Council has been absorbed into the newly created Higher Education Funding Council, which means that they are getting a larger share of the higher education financial cake. Their rise in total numbers of students has exceeded that of the universities and they are on a successful wave.

Polytechnics were sometimes considered the 'poor relation' to the universities and with this patronizing attitude there was some difficulty in attracting students. Part of the trouble was that they came from a rainbow of different traditions. The Polytechnic of the South Bank, for example, was formed in 1970 by the amalgamation of four colleges of different types, the oldest being the Borough Polytechnic founded in 1892. The main campus is at the Elephant and Castle and the older polytechnic building houses the science and engineering faculties. Old and new traditions are juxtaposed. All the polytechnics have histories which conflict with the new traditions they are seeking to build.

But they are an essential part of the government's thrust; a thrust which echoes a report from Professor Roscoe, of Manchester University, which was submitted to the Royal Commission on Scientific Instruction in 1970. He deplored the serious harm that would come from separating polytechnics and universities: 'very great evils must result from this tendency to multiply institutions – a tendency springing, probably, from the difficulty of modifying old institutions to meet new wants'. Lord Crowther-Hunt in the 1960s had touched a sensitive nerve when he wrote in *The Structure and Governance of Higher Education* (1983): 'if, as academics, we cannot defend successfully what we do before politicians (most of whom, anyway, are intelligent men and women of good will) then we need to question very seriously indeed whether we should actually be doing it'.

What the polytechnics actually do is at the heart of the government's strategy in higher education as well as in accountability. The numbers of students on full-time courses has continued to rise since polytechnics were designated in their present form at Hatfield, Sheffield and Sunderland on 1 January 1969. Although they now receive the lion's share of government money, their early expansion was achieved without any significant increase in money for additional lecturers or resources. They are large and often complicated institutions on several sites, and deal with large sums of money. In the past they were tightly controlled by a variety of organizations but since independence was granted on 1 April 1989 they have developed new management structures, yet without the tight control being jeopardized in any way.

Ninety-eight per cent of polytechnics' work is in higher education. There is a ready response to national, regional and local needs. Increasingly, courses are being opened up for students without traditional entry qualifications. Most major centres of industry and population have access to at least one polytechnic. They are seen as centres of teaching and it is on this basis that they must be judged. The lecturers are generally well qualified both formally and through their work and industrial experience. If the government wants institutions that are cheaper to run than universities, cater for an increasing number of students, and are meeting directly the needs of the community, then the polytechnics achieve these demands in the academic and training areas effectively.

The major argument of the opponents of this expansion of polytechnic provision has always been that academic standards would fall. However, this now looks as though it has been misjudged, because the new strategy pays special attention to what is called quality assurance. It recognizes that the

> prime responsibility for maintaining and enhancing the quality of teaching and learning rests with each individual institution . . . At the same time, there is a need for proper accountability for the substantial public funds invested in higher education. As part of this, students and employers need improved information about quality if the full benefit of increased competition is to be obtained.

There are five ways in which it is proposed that quality can be assured: quality control, quality audit, quality assessment, validation, and accreditation. The last two will involve much hard work and some discontent, not because they are wrong but because they are breaking new ground. Validation will involve approval of courses for the award of degrees and qualifications. The essential comparisons with other institutions, especially the universities, are likely to mean considerable heart-searching.

The CNAA was previously responsible for the accreditation of degrees in polytechnics except in two cases, where this was undertaken by the local university. Under the new arrangements polytechnics will undertake their own accreditation and the precise regulations have not yet been finalized.

It is in the area of assessment that there will be greatest controversy because although this is now well established, a system will have to be created to ensure comparability of standards between one polytechnic and another; this is unlikely to be accomplished without difficulty.

However, it was clear that the funding of higher education had become the major issue when in a letter to the *TES* on 14 January 1992, the new chief executive of the Higher Education Funding Council, Graeme Davies, said that institutions could be financially rewarded for collaboration and rationalization which maximized resources. Although merging of institutions would be discouraged, 'broad cohorts' of regional co-operation would be rewarded. Such co-operation between universities, polytechnics and colleges would by 'multi-levelled, involving mobility of students and staff while sharing, for example, libraries, laboratories, and equipment'.

Implicit in the letter, and in all the new plans for the reorganization of higher education, was the axiom that however public money was distributed, the spending of it would be fully accountable. Accountability had become the heart of reform as well as control. If a polytechnic was prepared to act in certain predetermined ways it would stand a good chance of getting money. Having obtained the money, it would have to account for the way it was spent – but it would get the money if it obeyed the rules.

In spite of the expressed wish on the part of Graeme Davies for collaboration between all places of higher education, it is a fair assumption that the opposite will happen, and that there will be increased competition. It remains to be seen whether this would be to the advantage of polytechnics.

Part of the problem of public funding is not just that there is not enough money to go round but that there is a never-ending struggle for private money as well. Competition has meant that there are far too many academic institutions chasing an ever-dwindling group of businesses and trusts willing to help. Unless careful steps are taken to monitor the whole competitive scene, the situation could get out of hand and reduce to absurdity the advantages of rivalry in a more friendly context.

COLLEGES

Twenty-eight colleges were transferred from local authorities to the control of the HEFC in 1992. These included some colleges of higher education like Ealing, some colleges of education like Charlotte Mason, and some art colleges like Loughborough College of Art and Design. They varied in size; the largest was the Dorset Institute of Higher Education, and the smallest the Royal Northern College of Music. Other colleges, such as the Camborne School of Mines and the Norwich School of Art, had the choice to transfer from local authorities. There was a third category of voluntary colleges – religious foundations like King Alfred's, Winchester, Newman College, Birmingham, and St Martin's, Lancaster. Some of these were closely connected with a university; for example St Martin's had links with Lancaster, Homerton College with Cambridge, and Christ Church College with Canterbury. Finally there was a group of grant-aided colleges, including

Goldsmiths' College, Shuttleworth Agricultural College and the Royal Academy of Music.

The most important point about these disparate colleges was that they *were* disparate, and the attempt to place them within the fold of one funding organization was an attempt to be administratively fair. The only strong criticism levelled against the plan was that it was an attempt on the part of the central government to make the colleges 'grey'. This was soon discounted. Anybody who seriously thought that the Royal College of Music, or the Writtle Agricultural College, could become anything other than that which they themselves wanted to be has no knowledge of these institutions.

Much of the criticism of the new plans to organize higher education has come from the universities. There has been much less opposition from the rest of the sector.

TEACHER TRAINING: THE RADICAL SOLUTION

Within the whole area of higher education, one of the most dramatic changes is soon to come in the field of teacher training. Apart from the days of the old pupil-teacher system, the training of future teachers has always required an extended course of theory, whether in a university department of education or in a college of education. Time has always been spent in a variety of schools but most of the time was in the education department. This is now going to change; the largest part of training time in the future will be spent in schools. Schools where student teachers will spend 80 per cent of their time will be designated 'partner schools', and students will be trained by experienced teachers. The schools will be chosen on the basis of academic results, numbers of pupils staying on, truancy rates, and the destinations of school-leavers. Responsibility will pass out of the hands of universities and colleges and into the schools, or at least some of them.

Newspaper comments made this seem the most sensational piece of educational news in the whole revolutionary educational package. The *Observer* declared: 'Teachers in uproar over training axe'. A more restrained *Independent* commented: 'Teachers to get lesson in not being boring'. 'Teachers trained on the cheap,' thought *The Times*, and the *Times Higher Educational Supplement* (*THES*) published a thoughtful article called 'Back to the future?'

All of these articles made the same points with varying degrees of dramatic effect. Is teaching a craft? Or is it part of the wider field of education and therefore an intellectually valid discipline like medicine? The new proposals may succeed in marginalizing the trendy left teacher but may not succeed in making a fundamental shift in professional power. They do give schools a clear role in teacher training but will they succeed in involving the whole school and not just an elite of senior teachers? It was thought that the new system would be cheaper, but this must be too optimistic; it is more likely that it will actually cost more, with the old training institutions refusing to retire gracefully and the schools now doing most of the work and needing extra money to do it. Innovation is always expensive.

The Universities Council for the Education of Teachers has raised several issues with the Secretary of State including their fears that the partnership between schools and training institutions will be unequal and will therefore raise some disturbing problems. This is an interesting comment in view of the fact that the inequality in the past was so transparently unacceptable to the teaching profession that the training courses in both university departments and colleges of education had become a sick joke. Barry Hugill, education correspondent of the *Observer*, condemned the new proposals forcefully on 5 December 1991: 'It's slick, it's glib, and it's wrong. Over the past few years schools have been turned upside down, inside and out and back to front without any noticeable improvement in standards.' Still, perhaps the government has got to the source of the lingering problem in reforming the training of teachers. The HMI thought the 'prime purpose of schools . . . is to teach pupils, not to train students' (*Independent*, 5 January 1992). To whom would the new training be accountable – the profession or the government? The professional unions and associations seem quite unable to understand the power that has suddenly fallen into the hands of their members. They do not appear to understand that if they only allow teachers to grasp the reforms in a constructive and creative way the profession can control the training of the people who enter it and thus genuinely control standards for the first time. John Sutton, General Secretary of the Secondary Heads Association (SHA), said implementation of the plan would mean that thousands of pupils would be taught by students. Nigel de Gruchy, General Secretary of the

NAS/UWT, said the Minister had ruined a good idea by pushing it to excess. Doug McAvoy, General Secretary of the NUT, did not consider that enough money had been allowed to provide the extra teachers required. Sadly, their comments highlight a missed opportunity.

The reforms do pose a serious set of problems arising out of the practical element in the BEd. degree. The scheme includes undergraduates taking this degree and this involves reducing the length of the course from four years to three. The *THES*, in an article on 10 January 1992, considered this the main battleground. The writer felt that a degree which provided students with both a general higher education and a solid subject base would over-emphasize practical classroom skills at the expense of the other equally important objectives of the course.

Chapter 5

Schools: National Curriculum, Children and Parents

The three parts of this chapter are closely interconnected although on the face of it they deal with what appear to be separate issues. The National Curriculum currently dominates every classroom, and directly affects every child, in every school. It is the recipe for education, the 'given' element of the country's requirements at school-age level, and the compulsory part of the teacher's commitment. When it has been completed there is not much left, although there is still enough for the school, and principally the governors, to have some influence.

The children are the centre of this – not because the plans are 'child centred', in the old-fashioned sense of that phrase, but because it is impossible, even today, to have any plans for a school education that does not start with the child. The new curriculum lays down certain essential subjects that must be taught and also specifies that they should be taught in particular ways and at certain stages. The third part of the chapter looks at the new and more important role given to parents, not only in relation to their place on governing bodies, but also how the school is more responsive to parents' needs. The section on choosing a school focuses more closely on the way in which parents and children react over education.

THE NATIONAL CURRICULUM

'Schools revolution on the way' was the headline in the *Daily Mail* on 28 September 1991. The article added that 'accountability and information [are] the two great principles of any modern society'. These comments relate to the publication of league tables which put the exam results of schools in rank-order but it could as easily have applied to the introduction of the National Curriculum, the single most important instrument used by the government to get to the heart of the educational process – the classroom.

The Education Reform Act 1988 was a major piece of legislation which had quickly followed two earlier Acts, and was more far reaching than either of them because it introduced the National Curriculum. This sought to determine the precise content and structure of education between the ages of 5 and 18. It struck at the very heart of the time-honoured freedom and independence which British teachers had always enjoyed and jealously guarded; this was an undefended inheritance, because it had never had to be justified. At the same time the 1988 Act contained elements which would make teachers, heads and governors answerable for what was taught in schools.

The National Curriculum makes a distinction between core subjects (English, maths, science and religious education) and foundation subjects (history, geography, technology, music, art, physical education and modern foreign languages). Each child is to be assessed at four Key Stages, which correspond to particular age groups:

Key Stage 1   age   7
         2   11
         3   14
         4   16

There are also attainment targets. These are not the same as assessment and can be measured at any age. In addition there are cross-curriculum dimensions, skills and themes. The dimensions include personal and social education, equal opportunities, multicultural education, and European awareness. The skills include observation, numeracy, communication, information judgement, interpersonal relationships, decision-making and problem-solving, research, physical and practical dexterity, and creative imaginative thinking. The themes are environmental education, economic and industrial understanding, education for citizenship, health education, and careers education and guidance. This long string of topics shows that control over what goes on in schools has been quite significantly increased. With that control came a demand that all people in schools, from the youngest child to the chairman, should be accountable. This is not a value judgement but a description; the outcry from many teaching organizations was vociferous. The Secretary at the time of the introduction of the new curriculum, John MacGregor, expressed his own belief succinctly on BBC Radio's Jimmy Young programme: 'we will be seeing what they have actually learned and not just what they've been taught.' He went on: 'You want to concentrate on the basics, which is what we're doing, and in a way with which the schools can cope.'

The schools had found it difficult to cope because all these new perspectives had come so soon after the introduction of the General Certificate of Secondary Education (GCSE), a single exam which had replaced O-levels and CSEs. This had immediately required the development of new styles of teaching, including continuous assessment, and the introduction of substantial individual project work. Many teachers had not adjusted to this when they were faced with yet another set of changes. For teachers, the most conservative element in society, this was a swift divorce from the cosy unconstructive grumbles of the past. The teachers may have been correct in their outrage, and perhaps the speed of change was unthinking, but it certainly increased the influence of the central authority.

It is hard to be clear about the reactions to the National Curriculum. The Annual Report from Her Majesty's Inspectors of Schools (1989–90) had some interesting comments. They wrote that in 1989–90 a lower proportion (28 per cent) of the work was of poor quality than in the previous year. They suggested that the benefits of the GCSE had become more clear and that the exam was now firmly established, with a 2.2 per cent increase in the proportion achieving grades A to C compared with the old GCE/CSE exams. Schools had been able to cope better with the welter of new initiatives caused by the introduction of the National Curriculum if they had been able to build on existing good practice through previous experience with GCSE or TVEI (a mechanism for enhancing and enriching the development of technological and vocational education in schools). Perhaps most importantly, HMI clearly stated that 'the management of teaching and learning has also become more demanding and . . . the schools require better guidance'.

It was clear that a variety of problems were being thrown up by the educational revolution. GCSE boards were being criticized for representing different standards. The monitoring body set up to prevent such differences was the School Examinations and Assessment Council but there had been some evidence that they had tolerated unacceptably fluctuating standards. The Junior Education Minister Tim Eggar also suggested that some of the questions set were too easy and he ordered the boards to look at these more carefully, in case there had been a deliberate attempt to bridge the gap between the GCSE and the National Curriculum. It was mentioned that the long-term future of the GCSE might be in jeopardy because the National Curriculum would provide all the testing that would be required.

It is a matter of significance that the government chose to do two things at once: to increase the centralization of education, and to seek to make education more accountable. It is perfectly easy to separate the two but there is an argument which suggests that local education authorities had become impossible to control from a financial as well as an ideological angle. At the same time there was growing unease in the country about standards in many areas of education; most allegations may have been untrue, but they were difficult to contain unless the government was prepared to take the kind of radical action which it was taking in so many other parts of national life. The idea of increased centralization was a major departure from the British tradition, but it was clearly a way of effectively controlling the kinds of change that would otherwise have been impossible to introduce. Having taken this bold step, it was much easier to make the reforms accountable by carefully monitoring them and by ensuring that built into the structure was a complicated system of tests which checked the progress of children and the effectiveness of teachers. Accountability made sure the innovations worked. When it was decided to simplify the tests for 7-year-olds, some teachers thought it was the Achilles' heel of the whole design. But critics underestimated the political acumen of a government which at that time had been in office for over ten years. The truth is that one alteration on a point of detail neither alters the basic structure of the educational reforms nor chips at the necessity, as the government sees it, for making that structure accountable. There will be other changes as the shape unfolds.

What is accountability expected to bring? Is it just a method of controlling the curriculum or is it more than that? Could there have been any other way of introducing a system of testing all children? These three questions are worth considering.

The benefits are total control, total knowledge of what is going on, and a greater chance of a reduction in costs. If it is thought important to compare the progress of a child on Merseyside with a child in Sevenoaks then there is now the machinery to enable this to be done. It also means that every teacher in the land can have his or her teaching monitored. It means that the teacher on Merseyside who wants to spend all his time teaching Greek will not be allowed to do so, nor will the fanatical sociology teacher in Sevenoaks be allowed to be lop-sided.

Is it more than a method of controlling the curriculum? Time will tell, but at the moment it looks as though there will be a whole set of other developments, such as teacher assessment, more sophisticated training methods, and greater collaboration between schools on inter-curriculum matters. Another important question is whether the curriculum is actually being controlled. The working parties in the different subjects did not always obey the guidelines they had been set and some, like history, still disagree. But it is fair to claim that there is now a much more unified pattern than there has ever been.

Is this the only way of testing children? Clearly there are a variety of other options but the proposals did start a process which can be refined. It has already been made clear that changes are possible and that the first set of proposals can be altered. Therefore one would expect that it will be possible to continue to correct imperfections. There is a wealth of expertise in the education world concerning assessment and testing.

On Monday, 21 October 1991, Jack Straw, the Shadow Secretary of Education, opened an article in *The Times*, 'Testing and assessment are central to the learning process. Every time a teacher checks a piece of written work by a child and offers praise or a suggestion for improvement, testing and assessment are taking place.' He went on to maintain that judgements should be checked externally, 'to help maintain a consistent standard'. He continued later in the same article, 'what we want to see is schools' effectiveness measured – or to use a fashionable market analogy – the "education value added" which a school creates.' I think the last jargon phrase means something like what used to be known as the hidden parts of the school curriculum and later came to mean all those parts of a school which are not assessed by standard mechanisms. These are so often what gives a school its distinctive character. The 'education value added' in Jack Straw's article highlights the very thing which it is difficult to include in the concept of accountability. He describes the analysis of this kind of information as 'one of the central problems of education' and concludes: 'there is no single truth about testing, no Holy Grail'.

What is already clear is that the National Curriculum is creating a whole range of new problems. Some quickly emerged with the implementation of the Education (Schools) Act of 1992 which said that the purpose of publishing examination results is to 'assist parents in choosing schools for their children', and to 'increase public awareness of the quality of the education provided by the schools concerned'.

The first national tables showing schools' performance in GCSE examinations were published in November 1992. Tim Hames, Fellow of Pembroke College, Oxford, writing in the *Mail on Sunday*, said the tables had 'sent a shockwave through the nation's education system'. One of the points made in his article, 'Tables turned on 30 years of secrecy', is that although these examination statistics and others like them have been known for years it is only now that they are being shared. He welcomes the emergence of the 'genie of information [coming] out of the bottle', and claims that 'these tables will shift power towards parents, students, successful teachers and successful schools'.

The league tables were not universally welcomed. David Woodhead, national director of the Independent Schools Information Service (ISIS) said: 'we always advise parents that exam results illustrate only one aspect of a school's success, and should be seen in the context of everything else it does'. The National Commission on Education made a comparable comment about National Curriculum attainment tasks. 'By themselves, examination results do not show a school's "added value". They do differ from one school to the next, but the pupil intakes also differ. "Added value" is the boost that a school gives to a child's previous level of attainment . . . Raw test and examination scores do not measure this gain and should be accompanied by an assessment of the contribution a school makes to its pupils' progress.'

Keith Howard, head of Queen Mary's Walsall, which had the best combined GCSE and A-level results of all English state schools, was also concerned about the tables. He wrote to Baroness Blatch, an Education Minister, complaining that the new curriculum beyond the age of 14 was too prescriptive and that the tests at 14 were 'a bureaucratic monster in the making'. She replied that schools had a 'significant element of flexibility already' and should organize the curriculum to suit their own requirements.

Much of the comment on competition and increased structure in education was not a surprise. An article in the London *Evening Standard* on 1 December 1992 raised the sensitive question of pupils being expelled because their disruptiveness was lowering the overall standard of school results. The consequence of a 'market-led emphasis on producing decent exam results to show prospective parents' was that unruly pupils were seen as a serious handicap to the attainment of that objective. Eric Forth, the Education Minister with particular responsibility for schools, has proposed that schools should be fined if too many pupils are excluded. The *Standard* says this isn't enough. 'There's got to be a reform in the entire educational culture' because, the article continues, 'a school system that can only cope with the agreeable children of supportive parents isn't worth having'. Nigel de Gruchy, as reported in the *Observer* of 15 December 1991, commented: 'the Minister was ruining a good idea by pushing it to excess; teachers cannot teach, and at the same time, act as prison warders'.

The Education Secretary, John Patten, decided that underachieving schools at the bottom of the GCSE league table should be inspected by the newly privatized school inspectors. These would be under the control of OFSTED, the Office for Standards in Education. Patten said, 'I am convinced that the more frequent and rigorous new inspection arrangements by the independent OFSTED will bring much-needed help to children in difficulty.' He saw the league tables as the 'historic turning point' in the debate on classroom standards.

CHILDREN

'Shameful' wrote the *Mail on Sunday* on 15 December 1991. 'Scandal in our schools' was the comment of the *Sunday Times* at the same time, and two months later it claimed: 'French teachers give Britain a lesson.'

These comments, and many others, described the publication of the league tables already mentioned. These will eventually become important and measurable ways of judging the progress of children. They will soon exist for all age groups and then a comparison can be made throughout the country of the state of achievement by all school pupils. The first tests for 7-year-olds were held in 1992, the tests for 14-year-olds were planned (but generally not carried out) for 1993, and those for 11-year-olds are planned for 1994.

DES publicity made a special point of emphasizing the national tests at the ages of 7, 11, 14 and 16. 'The results of these tests will be reported to you [the parents] so that you can follow your child's progress and work with the teachers to help that progress along' (DES, 1992a, p. 2). This is part of the general principle that there will be checks on children's progress through the National Curriculum at every stage. In addition to the tests there are regular progress checks, which are measured against national targets. It is hoped that the combination of clear targets and national tests will ensure that teachers have the highest expectation of their pupils, standards will be raised, pupil mobility will be easier, and that 'you, as a parent, can hold your child's school to account for the progress your child is making and for the standards of the school generally' (ibid., p. 7).

The results of the first national tests for 7-year-olds were surprising. Twenty-eight per cent of children tested could not read or recognize the first three letters in the alphabet. Twenty-six per cent could not do the simplest of sums, such as multiplying five by five. These individual tests were grouped into the respective LEAs, which were then put into rank-order.

The *Sunday Times* extracted some of the questions which the children had been asked to answer:

- Find the difference between seven and three.
- If six pencils are taken from a box of 10, how many are left?
- Work out the change from 30p when two cakes costing 15p and 6p are bought.
- How many jam rolls costing 40p can be bought for £3.20?
- If you had three £1 coins plus six 1p coins, how would it be written?
- What is half of eight?

- Name as many standard units as possible used to measure milk and water, length, the weight of an object and time.
- Add 5+2, 4+3, 1+6 and 6+4.
- Subtract 10−3, 7−2, 8−4, 6−3.

But the real question which had to be answered was which part of the child's whole development was tested by the tests. This is not to imply that the tests were without value, but they measured only a fragment, however important, of the child's total abilities.

Who was a child answerable or accountable to? Was it the parent, the teacher, the other children, or the religious group to which the child belonged?

There is no doubt that the home, including the parents, has the most powerful influence of all. That is not to say that the child is accountable to it. Much teenage behaviour over sex, dress and personal hygiene seems to flout every kind of parental authority. There is a sense in which parents only exist to be disobeyed. And yet there is no doubt that the influence of the parents, for good or ill, is dominant.

It is a time-honoured speculation whether teachers have more or less authority and status in the present day. What is beyond doubt is that many pupils feel they must prove themselves to their teachers. They are often more accountable to them than to anyone else. On 19 January 1992 the *Sunday Times* published a report of research into a comparison between British and French teaching methods. The burden of the newspaper article was that the rigorous way the French teach the three Rs was in sharp contrast to the more 'playschool approach' of the British. The point of quoting this research was not to revive the old debate about two sharply contrasted teaching styles but to highlight the priority the two groups give to the personal development of the child they teach. One in three British teachers interviewed by the researchers believed more in abstract targets which have less to do with basic skills, in contrast to the French teachers, two-thirds of whom regarded the teaching of the basic skills as fundamental to their work. Consequently, I believe, French teachers would put themselves into a significantly more accountable position with their pupils. A French child might feel completely answerable to the teacher; a British child might like the teacher very much but feel independent and not accountable at all. It might be enjoyable to go on a nature ramble or a visit to the British Museum, but most British teachers would not insist on any measurable response to the experience, and the child would almost certainly not feel accountable for having seen a butterfly.

There is also considerable pressure from a child's peer group. Children are affected by other children, usually their school friends, and they conform and relate to each other. This is one form of accountability, and often a powerful one. Children feel that they have to explain to their neighbours the reasons why they are doing something, or wearing something, or belonging to something; group pressure can be a very real influence on a child.

It would be inappropriate to ignore the religious influences on a child. It is why some children, for example Muslims, wear different clothing in school. It is why some Christian children cross themselves, or why Jewish boys wear different headgear. All these are outward signs of a relationship the child has with a particular religious group, and there are many more indications. But it is the spiritual obligation which makes children accountable for many of their actions and it is one about which they are most sensitive.

In a speech by Cardinal Hume at the North of England Conference in Newcastle in January 1990, he referred to a passage from a document addressed to Catholic teachers in France:

> God speaks gently to children, often without words, the natural creation provides the vocabulary – leaves, clouds, flowing water, a shaft of light. It is a secret language, not to be found in books. One sees a child pause suddenly in the midst of some activity, brought to a silent contemplation of some natural object or living creation or picture. . . . Here is the quality of looking and listening which brings him close to God, invoking in one act both the concreteness and the mystery of the world of things. The task of the religious teacher is to go beyond the admiration of the poet and the question of the philosopher as to the 'how' of things and allow the child to find the bond linking him with the 'who' – God the Creator.
>
> (Hume, 1990, p. 11)

Earthly considerations can shatter this childlike reality. Are children thrown by the regular presence of parents in a school? It is an unanswerable question, but it is an important one. Has the battery of school reform, which seeks to give parents a fair deal, actually resulted in the child getting less than before? Many can remember childhood occasions when parents came to the school and the acute embarrassment they brought. Now some adults tell us children love their parents to come and to be part of the running of the school and to involve themselves. This could be true of some junior children in a primary school who feel lost and lonely away from their mother's knee. But as the child gets older I seriously wonder whether the intrusion of parents is welcomed by the modern teenager and whether it is not the cause of as much embarrassment as ever. Perhaps for children the involvement of mum and dad is not so welcome, but it certainly increases the accountability of the offspring.

PARENTS

In an article on the Parent's Charter, 'Parents win new deal on schools,' commented the *Daily Telegraph* on 28 September 1991. 'Power points,' commented the *Guardian*, in a discussion of the power of parents on 16 July 1991. 'Labour sets out school rules for parents' was the headline in the *Independent* on 11 September 1991. 'Labour steals a march on parents' rights,' wrote David Tytler in *The Times* on the same day.

All the newspapers were writing about the different ways in which parents were being considered by the government and were being wooed by the other parties. What was so different about the new attitude to parents?

Not so long ago the general concern was that schools were too forbidding for parents to enter. Teachers and heads were considered unapproachable and most parents felt intimidated when they entered the school. To complain to the head about some aspect of the school or the treatment of a pupil was like going to get the cane. The fence or wall around the school was often seen as the frontier which separated the child's life from the outside world. It was all off-putting.

There was also a general mystery, concern or distrust of the subject matter in the class lessons. The new maths was unintelligible even for parents who had considered themselves good at arithmetic. Few teachers seemed to be at all interested in paying attention to spelling during English lessons. History seemed to be more concerned with the Piltdown Man than with what Wellington did at Waterloo. It was confusing. Worse than that, it had become impossible to help with children's homework, which reduced a contribution to children's development that had once been one of the most effective ways for parents to keep in contact during some formative years. It might have been difficult to get to grips with your child's friends but there was always that part of the evening when it was possible to have a quiet chat about important matters in the guise of explaining long division. The sums were unimportant but the chat was invaluable. Nowadays long division is no longer taught.

There was a longer-term severance, however, of the school from the family recollection. When schools were reorganized into a comprehensive pattern all types of local schools would be absorbed. The reasons for this were threefold. First, comprehensives were thought to be more economic; this proved to be largely untrue but it was a sincerely held belief in the 1960s. Second, it enabled a reasonably sized sixth form to exist if there were enough junior forms, and therefore it was necessary to ensure that there was a grammar-school-sized intake alongside one the size of a secondary modern. Third, it made administration easier if the LEA dealt with a smaller number of large schools; they could more simply impose a common set of policies and more tightly control the zoning of children, another form of power.

This wholesale reorganization destroyed the family tradition of attending the local institution. The school that grandfather went to was no longer in existence, whether it had been a grammar, technical or secondary modern school. The memory of particular classrooms or playgrounds was all that was left; and those who think that such nostalgia is either not important or that it only concerns the beautiful cricket fields of a country school underestimate the powerful treasury of childhood dreams. For parents, such change cuts them off from the nurturing of their children. Sadly, such talk is far from the reckoning of the administrators who are largely responsible for the planning of educational changes and they usually dismiss these arguments as sentimental twaddle.

When the *Daily Telegraph* described the Parent's Charter in a leader on 28 September 1991 as 'a landmark in the long process of unfastening the grip of the educationalists by giving parents a greater involvement in their children's schooling' it was taking a clear stand on the government's attitude to the place of parents. The Charter itself, published in 1991, was distributed free and aroused wide comment on the grounds that it was a political document and should therefore not be distributed through non-political maintained schools. Some LEAs and some schools would not send it to parents and instead told them that they could collect a copy from the school office.

The Charter described four new plans:

(1) annual written reports 'on your child's progress';
(2) regular reports by independent inspectors on the strengths and weaknesses of 'your school';
(3) published tables so that 'you can compare the performance of local schools';
(4) independent panels of assessors which hear parents' appeals if 'they do not get the school they want for their child'.

It also included quite specific pieces of advice about the role of parents in the education of their children. The Charter 'will help you to become a more effective partner in your child's education', and 'you will want to play a full part in it at every stage'. Clearly there were to be no frontiers constructed between the government and parents.

The Labour Party had issued a comparable document in September 1991, before the DES pamphlet was issued. Called *Parents' Partnership*, it stated: 'We are keen to develop among parents a greater sense of shared responsibility towards their child's school and education', and went on to recommend home/school partnership agreements, which were already operating in some schools. Under arrangements of this kind, parents would promise to take a positive attitude to school over attending meetings, checking homework, monitoring television viewing, ensuring adequate sleep, and telling the teacher of anything that might affect the child's performance in school. In return the school would promise that the class teacher would be willing to talk over any problem at a mutually convenient time, and ensure that the child was educated to the best of his/her ability.

Joan Sallis, President of the Campaign for the Advancement of State Education, expressed doubts about the Labour plan. 'A contract of mutual obligations is going to make some people feel even worse parents. If you live in a bed and breakfast and have to beg in Euston Station then you haven't a lot of chance of abiding by a school contract. The school should come nine-tenths of the way to meet your difficulties' (quoted in the *Guardian*, 11 September 1991).

Jack Straw, Shadow Secretary of Education, claimed that 'in their market model of education the Conservatives see parents as "consumers" and rather passive ones at that. In contrast we will give parents effective rights, including the right to action against a local authority, and to a public enquiry into any plan to close a school.'

The Liberal Democrats' charter, *Citizens' Britain*, included an important section on education which proposed the introduction of free nursery education for all, the expansion of higher education and the creation of consumer panels to monitor the local education service.

An important comment on the government proposals came from Cardinal Hume in his speech in January 1990. He sought 'to make connections, to show the relevance and inner coherence of a particular vision of life', and he began by quoting verbatim the Education Reform Act 1988: 'The curriculum, it said, should be one which "promotes the spiritual, moral, cultural, mental and physical development of pupils".' He went on to state that the curriculum should prepare pupils 'for the opportunities, responsibilities and experiences of adult life'. It is a long and thoughtful speech, in which the Cardinal refers to parents:

> We ought never to forget that parents are the primary educators of their children. Their physical, psychological, emotional and spiritual imprint is something the child carries through life as a burden or a blessing. Attitudes are being continually and subtly transmitted to the next generation. What takes place in the home is vital and far outweighs in importance the growing power of parents in the running of the school. The influence of parent governors is to be welcomed as well as the involvement of PTAs in the life of the school but it does not stop there.

The *Daily Telegraph* in its article on 28 September 1991 did not agree with one part of this speech which had criticized the fostering of competition among schools and the introduction of commercial concepts as an 'undesirable and dangerous development'. The newspaper found it hard 'to understand the logic of this'. 'Schools should not be judged solely on their exam results, but to argue that for this reason they should not be published is to suggest that parents are incapable of making up their own minds about what constitutes a good school.' By contrast, the *Daily Mail* on the same date welcomed the reforms of the Secretary of State for Education, Kenneth Clarke, and believed the 'foundations are being laid for reversing the decline of recent years'. It went on: 'accountability and information – the two great principles of any modern society – have been denied to families and taxpayers alike'.

Chapter 6

The White Paper of July 1992 and Grant-maintained Schools*

'A pattern of chaos' (*Guardian*)
'Schools: is out in?' (*Sunday Telegraph*)
'To go or not to go?' (*TES*)
'Escape from the town hall's grip' (*Daily Mail*)
'Patten seizes control of state education' (*The Times*)
'Opting out for less democracy' (Jarvis in *The Times*)
'Private schools to opt in' (*TES*)

These were some of the headlines which described the announcement of the government's White Paper on Education announced on 28 July 1992 and called *Choice and Diversity*. Grant-maintained (GM) schools had been introduced in 1989. Already there were over 250 of them. They had quite significant independence, including control over their own budgets, pupil entrance and appointment of staff, and parents had a majority on their governing bodies. All this was permitted if a majority of parents voted in favour of the idea. They were not, however, allowed to change the nature of the school. Money came directly from central government.

The White Paper was the final part of the government's reform of education. Its main points were very clear:

(1) A national funding agency for grant-maintained schools would share responsibility for admissions in areas where more than 10 per cent of pupils had opted out.

---

*This chapter was written before the legislation was enacted in 1993 and therefore does not take account of any changes that occurred during its passage through Parliament.

(2)   Applications for grant-maintained status were to be speeded up. Primary schools were to be enabled to opt out in 'clusters'; voluntary bodies should be helped to found GM schools; independent schools could apply to be grant-maintained.

(3)   The Secretary of State was given considerable powers of intervention. Where a school was faltering, management teams would be empowered to step in and such schools could then opt out without parental ballot. He also had the power to remove governors from GM schools.

(4)   Some schools could change their character when they opted out and, for example, concentrate on technology, languages or business studies.

(5)   The National Curriculum Council and the School Examinations and Assessment Council were to merge.

(6)   Local education authorities were to lose many of their functions and power was increasingly to be delegated to schools. Nevertheless the LEAs would retain functions in special needs, transport and monitoring attendance, and compete to provide services to GM schools.

(7)   On morality and pastoral care, the authorities were to speed up the review of religious education, crack down on truancy and, in the classroom, put greater emphasis on right and wrong.

This is a very condensed version of a 64-page document, which had been partly written by John Patten himself. Most of the Tory press were in favour. Comments such as this from the *Daily Mail* were common: 'Yesterday's White Paper is both heartening and historic. It ushers in a new era for pupils who will be tested, teachers who will be assessed and schools which will be inspected with rigour and regularity.' But reaction in the profession was frequently opposed to the idea, and at best reserved.

The NUT's president said: 'wherever he [the Secretary of State] fears that democracy may be heard, he seeks to silence it. But by so doing the government can no longer hide its responsibility for what happens in our schools' (Matthew d'Ancona quoting Doug McAvoy in *The Times*, 29 July 1992). He criticized the marginalization of local education authorities and the Secretary of State's new right to remove governors.

Nigel de Gruchy, General Secretary of the NAS/UWT, while

welcoming the merger of the examination and curriculum councils and the paying of attention to special needs, also commented that opted-out schools were not an educational panacea: 'GM schools were opting out of the LEA frying pan and into the funding agency fire' (ibid.).

Peter Smith, General Secretary of the Assistant Masters' and Mistresses' Association (AMMA), had commented just before the White Paper was issued that he would like there to be consultation on various issues; the White Paper covered most of his points. He had said that 'government by progressive revelation is just not good enough . . . Whatever view the government takes of local authorities, for them to be put to death by 1000 cuts is bad government'.

Chris Adamson, speaking for the Association of London Authorities, said that the government had to recognize that LEAs had a place. 'The proposals do not spell the end of the local education authority . . . in giving extra powers to LEAs to deal with failing schools, the government has had to recognise the value of a locally, democratically accountable network for schools.'

Margaret Morrissey of the National Confederation of Parent-Teacher Associations (NCPTA) considered that opted-out schools would receive preferential treatment. 'We believe the proposed new legislation will help and support GM schools and leave many others with little or no choice, and many in great threat of closure.'

The spokesperson on education for the Labour Party, Ann Taylor, considered the White Paper a recipe for local confusion. 'What we need is proper local co-ordination and proper local support for our schools. The government is wrong to pretend that you can squeeze the local authorities and somehow not create more problems.' At the Labour Party conference the following September she encouraged her party to make sure its governors were active in an anti-opt-out campaign. The party had made clear its opposition to opting out, and at the same conference, passed a motion opposing it in principle and practice. Also at this conference, Dennis Reed of NALGO (National and Local Government Officers Association) said it would rally the fight against the White Paper, which 'would mean the death of local authorities'. There was thus considerable hardening of the attitude of the Labour Party towards the opting-out proposals.

Various fears were caused by the proposals. Some, such as

Dennis Hatfield, General Secretary of the Society of Education Officers, in a letter to *The Times* expressed the view that schools might become selective. John Patten had already said that he had not had a single application to introduce a selective intake since taking office. The White Paper distinguished between academic selection and the identification of an aptitude for a particular specialization. His aim throughout the White Paper had been to 'extend choice and diversity'.

Nevertheless, the reduction in the powers and responsibilities of local authorities was explicit, and many commentators saw in the White Paper the eventual demise of LEAs. Even the obligation for councils to have an education committee was to disappear. This dramatic change in the local government of education led Fred Jarvis, formerly general secretary of the NUT, to fear that education would become more undemocratic, and he deplored the marginalization of the LEAs.

Some of the opposition to the schools that wished to opt out had been undemocratic too. Parents at Grangefield School, Stockton-on-Tees, were surprised when they discovered that NALGO had mailed anti-opt-out leaflets to parents of pupils from its Middlesbrough office; Labour-controlled Cleveland County Council ran a hostile article in its newspaper; and branches of the NUT and the NAS/UWT issued pamphlets declaring that teachers were opposed to opting out. When interviewed, Nigel de Gruchy declared that the government was spending freely to promote opting out so 'why shouldn't opponents do the same?'

The Times, in a highly critical leader on 29 July 1992, suggested that the reforms were the most dramatic since the war and that the White Paper did not create a free market in education. 'The need for centralisation is a mystery,' it continued and then claimed that the government 'has not thought through its search for diversity, parental choice, specialism and standards'. It concluded that 'British schools need time to recover from the inanities of the 1970s, not another blow for change – and certainly not a blow from the discredited sledgehammer of nationalisation'.

Was anybody, except the government, the Tory press, and Robert Balchin, secretary of the Grant Maintained Trust, in favour of the White Paper? All the speakers for all the institutionalized bodies were opposed to the reforms, or so they said. But the number of applications from schools to opt out rose rapidly. It was as though there was a groundswell of support from those who were keen to run the schools their children attended. Their educational horizon was limited, particular, and would only last for the duration of their children's schooling. But the support they gave to the new ideas was real and positive. It was a support which was linked with the most powerful pressure of all: the pressure of wanting the best for their children.

We will now consider the specific areas of the White Paper.

THE FUNDING AGENCY

This new statutory body will have up to 15 members appointed by the Education Secretary and drawn from various backgrounds. It will be responsible for the payment of grants, and for financial monitoring of GM schools. It will open regional offices as the number of opt-out schools demands them. It will have increasing responsibilities for rationalization of places in GM schools and for securing sufficient places and will set up a common formula for funding.

All of these proposals depend upon a significant increase in the number of schools opting out. The assumption was that the total number would increase fairly rapidly and all the early signs suggest that this is happening, although not at the rate the government originally expected. The problems that would arise if total numbers do not increase will be great. Professor Eric Bolton, echoing the *Guardian* headline about chaos, saw visions of chaos arising out of the White Paper. One of the things he said he feared, in a speech to the Council of Local Education Authorities in July 1992, was that as more power was assumed by central government, more would be delegated to the schools, which would then become increasingly motivated by self-interest.

Other observers were relieved that the funding of GM schools was to be regularized to accommodate their future expansion. It was also said that the Funding Agency would only be doing at a national level what LEAs had done for years, especially since the introduction of LMS. But the major difference would be a significant saving of money as well as the hope of increased fairness without education in schools being subject to the vagaries of local politicians.

GREATER POWERS FOR THE SECRETARY OF STATE

The chair and first chief executive of the newly established Funding Council are appointed by the Secretary of State for Education, who can regulate and guide the Funding Council and has general powers to confer additional duties on it. He has the power to send an education association into any school that is at risk and can set the remit of that association. He can set out common instruments and articles of government for opted-out schools. He can add two governors or institute procedures to close a school if a governing body is unsatisfactory. He can replace some or all first governors of ex-county GM schools. He can direct the Funding Agency, which implements the decisions of the Council, to come forward with rationalization plans within a specific time, arrange a local inquiry and make the final decision. He can rule on proposals by voluntary bodies to set up opted-out schools. He can appoint inspectors to lead public inquiries in closure and rationalization cases. He has the power to vary the standard number of pupils a school admits and control admissions where joint arrangements between the Funding Agency and the local authority are not possible. He can pay the governing body's expenses of promoting opting out and cover 'reasonable' legal costs of governing bodies arising out of holding an opting-out ballot or publishing proposals. He can reject a school's change of character or enlargement proposals while approving grant-maintained status. He can amend the agreed religious composition of the Standing Advisory Council on Religious Education once 75 per cent of pupils are in opted-out schools. He can permit special schools to apply to opt out. He can approve the appointment of a sponsor in voluntary-aided or GM schools after hearing about the financial and curricular benefits he or she would bring. He can create a network of technology colleges with business strongly represented on the governing body. He can allow technology colleges to opt out.

All these changes represent departures from the Butler Act of 1944 and increased the powers of the Secretary of State. *The Times* headline on the day of publication of the White Paper was: 'Patten seizes control of state education in schools' and the leader was entitled: 'State knows best'. It stated: 'this is a devastating vote of no confidence in local democracy'. It was – and perhaps local democracy had been asking for it for years.

LOCAL AUTHORITIES

The local authority would provide the Funding Agency with information, have the power to change the character or the age range of voluntary schools, be able to propose the establishment or closure of voluntary schools up to the point when 75 per cent of pupils were in opted-out schools, and to propose new schools if they are part of a major reorganization once the 75 per cent point is reached. They also had the power to force a school to accept a pupil, assess and statement special needs and send the child to the school named in the statement. They would be allowed to spend only a limited amount of money campaigning against GM proposals. They would be required to take in pupils with special needs and would no longer need the consent of the Secretary of State to send a special needs pupil to an independent school. They would be able to contribute towards governors' capital costs at voluntary-aided schools or colleges. They could appoint additional governors in 'at risk' schools and withdraw funds, and they would have to submit a report to the Secretary of State on the 'at risk' school within eight weeks. They would no longer be required to have an education committee.

These provisions represent not only the transformation of the LEAs but the seeds of their own demise. It was transparent that Patten was determined to take education out of the control of local politics and, for the most part, out of the control of local administrators. Perhaps the most telling proposal was the removal of the need for local authorities to have an education committee. The retention of responsibility for some of the services, and also for those schools which did not opt out, was seen as a temporary administrative convenience. Schools were no longer obliged to use any of the services offered by the LEA and those schools which did not seek to become GM schools would quite soon be in an untenable position.

Larry Goodband, chairman of the National Confederation of Parent-Teacher Associations, challenged the value of eroding the powers of LEAs. The White Paper: 'is good for parents of children in grant-maintained schools and those in LEAs not meeting their wishes. But for the majority in the middle, it offers nothing' (reported in *TES*, 7 August 1992). That was precisely the point. The proposals were only designed for the two groups outlined by

Mr Goodband. There was other opposition to this part of the White Paper.

The Society of Education Officers agreed to have talks with the National Confederation of Parent-Teacher Associations to 'consider how they can minimise the damaging aspects of the legislation' (reported in *TES*, 7 August 1992). Thirty-one LEAs were planning a publicity campaign to encourage parents to participate in any ballot about grant-maintained status and to oppose opt-out measures. Other groups have already been created between parents and councillors to act as watchdogs on the changes which are being proposed. At a fringe meeting of the Labour Party Conference, reported in the *TES* on 2 October 1992, Dennis Reed, the national officer for local government in NALGO, said the White Paper would mean the death of local education authorities and called the section on the future of the authorities 'one and a half pages of vindictive text'. Ann Taylor for Labour, however, is not totally pessimistic about the future of LEAs, because the White Paper recognizes their function and gives them new powers.

But the great groundswell of opposition from parents that official bodies had expected did not materialize. Nor was there any great opposition to the LEAs. Were parents interested in education?

PARENTS

The White Paper assumed that a majority of parents wanted a chance to vote about the status of the school their child went to and that they would vote in favour of GM schools. The number of applications by schools wishing to be considered for GM status is now on the rise after a slow start. The White Paper encouraged this, although it seems likely that a Conservative win in the last general election helped the applications along even more. Now schools will be given even more freedom by being able to change their character if they wish, and since the majority of the governing body is always parents this is a major step for parents. The White Paper also announced that schools which have been inspected should ensure that parents receive straightforward details of the inspectors' findings. These are not earth-shattering additions to parents' power but they are important because they do consolidate the existing parent power.

THE NEW BUREAUCRACY

The Funding Agency for schools has already been mentioned but it is not the only agency involved. Almost as important is the School Curriculum and Assessment Authority (SCAA) formed by the merger of the National Curriculum Council and the School Examinations and Assessment Council in 1993. The Education Secretary appoints a chairman and 15 members to monitor the curriculum and complete the introduction of testing. Education associations were also proposed in the White Paper. These are the small bodies appointed by the Education Secretary to take over management of 'at risk' schools if local authority rescue plans fail. Consisting of headteachers and managers, associations have the power to replace staff and propose school closures. Finally, the White Paper established special needs tribunals, which are regional panels appointed by the Education Secretary to arbitrate where parents believe the special needs of their children are not being met.

MORALS

The White Paper specified that schools should be instructed to teach values such as respect for people and property; honesty and consideration for others; trust, fairness and politeness. Pupils must be given a clear moral message and be taught the difference between right and wrong. Schools 'should not be value-free zones'. It was Brian Appleyard, writing in *The Times* on 29 July 1992, who claimed that 'the classroom was in the front line of the culture'. He meant that the current form of democracy has within it the seeds of its own destruction. If it becomes too liberal it destroys itself.

When John Patten says in the White Paper that he wants schools to teach the difference between right and wrong he runs the risk that it will be discussed into the ground and so not achieve the object he seeks. It might well be desirable to teach the difference between right and wrong if everybody concerned agreed on exactly what the words meant. The Secretary of State himself is a devout Roman Catholic, but the majority of teachers are not even Christian and even if they were they would probably not find the teaching of the difference between right and wrong any easier. One could insist in a primary school that stealing was wrong. Children, parents and all the staff could agree. But supposing the question was whether 14-year-olds should be allowed to buy condoms in school. On this issue the staffroom might be divided and all sides of the discussion could well be expressing sincerely held convictions about right and wrong.

Patten takes a tough line on truancy; rates of absence would have to be published to try and stamp out 'the journey from the street corner to the prison cell'. In the White Paper there was an obligation on local authorities to 'find alternative education' for pupils whose behaviour is persistently unacceptable.

But the White Paper also advocated that misbehaviour should not be tolerated:

> The problem is often at its worst in our inner cities or large housing estates, though there are beacon schools whose head teachers and governors have taken swift and effective remedial action. Unsurprisingly, these are the schools to which parents flock, whose walls bulge, and whose education is an object lesson.

The White Paper suggests that religious education should be reviewed. This will not be easy in a multicultural society. Already the Muslim parliament has applied for a government grant to support an existing independent Muslim school.

The Secretary of State clearly believes that the White Paper is what parents want. Much emphasis is placed upon failing schools; the Education Secretary plans to explain which they are and how they can be helped after they have been inspected. Surprising support came from Ann Charlton, a former local government officer for the Labour Party. In *The Times* of 2 August 1992 she wrote:

> children respect teachers who keep control, mark work, set tests and homework and enable them to gain qualifications. Parents would appreciate less jargon, more marking and homework, more setting, more openness on examination results, bad teachers being weeded out and discipline restored. . . . There is nothing unsocialist about such attitudes.

Much of this chapter is an attempt to come to terms with a legacy of low standards and unacceptable customs. It is to John Patten's credit that he has tried to deal with the real problems of morals, style and conduct even if he has left many loose ends and created even more problems than he has solved.

ADMINISTRATION

The proposed form of educational operations in the medium term gave the impression of instability. The essential structure was at two parallel levels. The one part concerned the new GM administration. The other part was the alternative organization, consisting of the LEAs running the remainder of the schools, which for one reason or another had not opted out. The first would be centrally controlled and financed directly by the DfE but initially it would be quite small. The other would be the existing organization of the LEAs. The two systems would run in parallel. In the short term this could lead to a variety of unnecessary problems but in the long term the number of grant-maintained schools would either have increased to make the GM organization a totally effective framework for all the secondary schools in the country or the GM schools would not have materialized and the LEAs, with some modifications, would have regained control and the power they had once possessed. So the bilateral administration contained a medium-term weakness from the start.

There was a comparable administrative unease about the arrangements for special needs provision. The proposed structure provided for a regional organization; the latter had much common sense about it because it allowed for children with special needs to be in close contact with those who could best help them. However, it did mean that there would have to be some form of standard statementing so that the recorded needs of specific children could be effectively transferred when required. But the necessary administration did involve standardization, comparability, efficiency and expense; it thus contained within it some instability.

There was also an implicit assumption that most of the proposals would be appropriate to inner city or suburban areas. Much legislation concerning education has always been concerned anyway with the larger towns and cities, and yet the proportion of children living in rural areas is high. An example of the difficulty which the White Paper would reveal is that primary schools are able to become opted-out schools if they group into clusters. This means that quite small village schools can have the advantages of being GM without losing the particular identity of which many are proud and which involve the local community to good effect. In rural areas, however, primary schools are not always situated geographically close enough to collaborate effectively. Furthermore, unless clustering is based on self-choice, which seems unlikely, there could well be friction from the start with primary schools in the same cluster not working in harmony with each other. Such clustering might work in the inner cities but it is fraught with problems in the country districts.

The most telling structural dilemma was that the proposals struck at the very heart of the comprehensive principle. This is partly because it was suggested that there should be greater diversity and specialization through the developing network of specialist technology schools, with City Technology Colleges at the centre. It was also because it was intended that LEA and GM schools should form partnerships to operate as GM and voluntary-aided technology colleges whose governing bodies would include individuals from the private sector and representatives of organizations.

But the inherent weakness was that these changes would almost certainly conflict with the comprehensive school monopoly. If this monopoly was to be challenged by widespread specialization then the changes would cost a great deal. They would also involve travelling long distances, probably wasting a good deal of time for students and teachers alike.

WILL THE WHITE PAPER BECOME LAW?

At the moment the White Paper is only a set of proposals and will have to be debated in parliament as a Bill before it becomes law. It is unlikely to be drastically amended, because it will be accepted by a clear majority of the Conservative Party. It embodies, consolidates and strengthens what has already been agreed in principle. It is the most recent major piece of legislation on education and in perfect accord with previous reforms. Nevertheless, it needs some refinement before it becomes law.

The relationship between central and local government needs to be more clearly delineated. The White Paper has been criticized for undervaluing the informal networks and activities which often form the heart of local government. If LEAs were encouraged to die, their death could mean the disappearance of much 'hidden' value built over years and the White Paper does not suggest how alternative systems might be created.

The whole area of financial arrangements needs attention. GM schools are to have a common funding formula; this means that the DfE will determine age weightings and the balance of resources between primary and secondary schools. The White Paper refers to a balancing adjustment in individual funding but this is as yet unspecified. In any case it is unlikely that the common funding formula will equate with an LEA's formula arrangements. This is probably one of the decisions which the Secretary of State will use to justify increased centralization, maintaining that it is about time financial allocations between LEAs should be made more equitable. It is precisely this unevenness which Patten wished to remove, so to claim it exists is to state the obvious.

The key area to be considered is the role of the LEA. The White Paper was quite unambivalent:

> The current review of the structure of local government will have a bearing on the way LEAs exercise their functions. As the number of GM schools increases, local authorities will need to consider carefully the most effective way of delivering their continuing responsibilities for education in the light of their particular circumstances. At present there are statutory obstacles which deny local authorities the organisational flexibility which they need to respond to the evolution of their education functions. The Government proposes to remove such obstacles, in particular the requirement to establish an Education Committee. Some local authorities may soon be in sight of no longer needing them.

The only way in which the majority of LEAs have begun seriously to evaluate their position is to count the number of individuals within them who have applied for jobs outside the cosy LEA cocoon; staff quickly discover that they are now being paid less. One of the questions which the central government is addressing and will have to continue to watch is the subtle and overt opposition to the proposals which the educational establishment and some of the local authorities are promoting. Obstacles are being placed in the way of some schools which try to opt out of local authority control and often, as the *Daily Mail* said on 11 October 1992: 'Mr Patten has blamed Labour Councils for preventing a flood of schools applying to opt out.'

Of all the government's attempts to introduce accountability, the White Paper on education must be seen as the main explanation not only of the financial implications but also of the need to create a system which makes all educational institutions more responsible. This is what makes the White Paper, and with it the subsequent law, central to an understanding of the government's determination to make education accountable.

GRANT-MAINTAINED SCHOOLS

These schools are one of the sharpest examples of accountability in action. They have already been mentioned in several places in this book, and we will now look at them more specifically. The government

> hopes that all schools will eventually become grant-maintained . . .
> The Government strongly believes that grant-maintained or GM status is best for state schools . . . They govern themselves: they run their own affairs and decide how to spend the money available to them.

The government could not have made their position clearer than they did with these words, taken from the leaflet which publicized the White Paper.

The new framework of GM schools was available to schools whose parents voted for them to leave their local authorities. It was the parents who took the decision, not the governors or the teachers, and the government was clear both that parents should decide and that they should do this by ballot. The parents had to apply, give their reasons, and then have formal approval for the change by the Department for Education. As soon as a school opts out it gets its own budget, which includes the share of what the LEA keeps for administration and providing services to schools. This money may be spent by the school as it thinks fit but it is under no obligation to purchase LEA services. The school no longer has to ask permission from County or Town Hall before it can spend money, a freedom which is meant to give a new sense of ownership and independence.

When there is a larger number of GM schools it is the Funding Agency for Schools which will be responsible for paying grants but will not be involved in the day-to-day running of a GM school. The Agency will share with the LEA the duty to secure sufficient secondary or primary places in any area where 10 per cent of pupils are in GM schools. The Funding Agency will discharge the duty by itself when 75 per cent of secondary (or primary) pupils in the LEA are in GM schools, though the LEA may be relieved of this responsibility well before that point is reached.

The Funding Agency will have 10 to 15 members to reflect the broad range of education and other experience, but they will be unelected and there are no arrangements for democratically elected members. Perhaps this will be arranged nearer the time when the Agency is actually in existence.

The transition to GM status will be eased with the removal of the second resolution of the governing body before a school proceeds to the parental ballot. The government will also give the governing body financial assistance so that it can explain how a school will benefit from opting out.

The opposition to GM schools was immediate but, in general, not well informed or clever enough to understand that the government had anticipated most of the objections. One example was the suggestion that GM schools would lose out financially when there were more of them. John Patten responded at once to this rumour and wrote directly to the headteachers and chairs of governors of all 24,000 schools in England and Wales about the 'misinformation' he believed was being put out by some local authorities about the risks of opting out. Mr Patten promised heads and governors that opted-out schools 'will continue to receive additional funding to reflect their additional responsibilities'. The *Daily Mail*, on 12 October 1992, accused opponents of the scheme to promote opted-out schools of 'bullying, petty-minded vindictiveness, and malicious lying'. It continues:

> most of the worst offenders have been the Labour-run councils in some of Britain's poorest areas where large sums of money have been spent trying to intimidate parents rather than enabling them to exercise their right to choose . . . But neither is every Conservative council a virtuous enthusiast for the policy. Many of the shire counties display similar, if more genteelly expressed, obduracy.

The Conservative Education Association, for example, released a highly critical response at the 1992 Conservative Party conference. They wrote: 'the government is nationalising the schools of England and Wales. . . . We believe it represents a massive and dangerous increase in the power given to central government.' Even the Church feared that the scheme would run the risk that church schools would lose their distinctive character, and 40 Roman Catholic bishops wrote to Mr Patten. They were also afraid that the proposals would lead to 'considerable imbalances in funding'.

The idea of grouping small schools into clusters received a mixed response but this could well be the innate conservatism of many of those involved. Some councillors thought it was an unworkable design and asked the Education Secretary to refine it. They did not think it would save money and feared it would cause problems of competition between the schools in the cluster. Molly Stiles, however, co-ordinator of the National Association for the Support of Small Schools, was very much in favour of the scheme and would fight to have the measure reinstated if it was threatened: 'I would be shattered if this happened. This is purely a case of the local authorities trying to hold on to their powers' (*Daily Telegraph*, 11 October 1992). Although she was speaking on behalf of only one group of schools one did have the feeling that much of the opposition in other areas had been motivated by the same dog-in-the-manger attitude. Throughout it all the Secretary of State remained calm, cogent and determined: 'It is very likely that in a good number of counties and metropolitan areas the local council may well be abolished. There may be some totally new framework,' he said in 1992. He went on: 'I have contempt for those who play on parents' fears.'

Chapter 7

The Teaching Profession

In one important sense the teacher has traditionally been one of the most accountable members of society. The teacher has been accountable to a board of governors who probably appointed and, at best, would know him or her. The teacher who did not feel accountable to all or any of the governors would be unusual. The teacher was certainly accountable to the head and would expect to answer for his/her actions in all parts of his/her work and life in school. When the headmaster asked to see you, you felt instantly accountable, even if the head was a pleasant person. Your sense of answerability might reach terror proportions if you knew you had done something wrong or if the head was an objectionable person. The head too was answerable to the staff with whom he worked, and this was never in doubt if one failed to stand in for an absent teacher. On other occasions, when the staff acted with one voice, a teacher felt answerable and accountable to the group. Similarly, teachers are answerable to the parents; no teacher could avoid realizing this during a parents' evening. Teachers were answerable to the local education authority in many ways in the days before LMS when a visit from the LEA adviser could cause fear; and answerable to the community, especially if the teacher worked in a village primary school, or as a PE adviser who wished to use playing space in the school for activities of the local community. Teachers were answerable to the pupils in the most telling respect of all because if teachers did not respond to the pupils sensitively they could use the ultimate weapon of being unruly in his classes.

This chapter will concentrate on three areas concerned with accountability which have recently been accentuated. They are pay, performance and partnership.

PAY

The discussion of this subject more than any other has usually devalued all those who have been particularly concerned with it. Whether it is to do with unions, employers or management, the consideration of pay has emphasized aspects of teaching which would have been better left unstressed. On the one hand, the profession has insisted that it is committed, hard-working and underpaid. On the other, teachers have consistently been attacked for adopting a 9 to 4 working day, enjoying long holidays sarcastically called the 'teachers' rest', and bleating and complaining about their pay. It has been an almost irreconcilable equation and few governments have seriously tackled the question of the morale of both teacher and parent.

Recently the balance of the equation has significantly changed because the demands of the National Curriculum have required many extra hours' work. Furthermore, the increasing power of parental interest in the routine organization of schools has led to much greater awareness on their part. This has not always meant that parents have approved the traditional stance of the teacher but it has led to greater knowledge of what the job involves.

Parental involvement in the profession has been most important in the move to grant-maintained status. Not only is it necessary for a majority of parents to agree with the new designation but once the school has opted out the parents must, by statute, be in a majority on the governing body.

In all these changes there has been a demand for greater accountability of teachers and it is often a demand that has been tinged with criticism. The teachers' unions may have steadfastly supported their members but the backwoodsmen among the parents, who are often the most silent but in the end the most influential, grabbed the power to interfere and control the teachers with alacrity.

Consequently it was not enough for teachers to be accountable to everybody under the sun. Now it became important for teachers to adjust to the idea that their pay would be related to performance. In July 1992, the Secretary of State, John Patten, said 'resources for performance-related pay should be found by devoting to that purpose an increasing proportion of the pay bill . . . through higher increases than would otherwise be the case'.

'Exam results may govern teachers' pay,' said *The Times* on 18 July 1992. The *Daily Mail*'s headline on the same day read: 'Teachers' Pay Linked to School Performance'. By 9 October 1992 the *TES* feared: 'performance pay open to manipulation'. The recommendations of the School Teachers' Review Body, published in October 1992, called for cash reserves to be paid to those schools whose performance improves from one year to the next. Such a performance-related pay (PRP) structure has always been dreaded by teachers' unions. The Review Body did concede that the proposed awards are 'crude', but hopes and believes they will form a suitable basis for refinement.

Measurements of performance will include exam results, National Curriculum assessments, truancy rates, and the destination of school-leavers. Schools would be penalized for poor teacher attendance or high pupil exclusion.

Teachers' unions have strenuously opposed PRP. In 1992 Doug McAvoy of the NUT said that 'the Review Body is now dancing to the government's tune', and feared that 'schools which are more advantageously financed to begin with would be favoured'. Nigel de Gruchy of NAS/UWT regarded the proposals as 'pedestrian and philistine: disputes over who gets what in the carve-up of the "performance bonus" could de-motivate many. These proposals run the risk of reducing education to a number-crunching exercise'. David Hart of the NAHT said the proposals, which include an additional task for heads in allocating the payments, 'would lead to further bureaucracy and centralization'. 'It's going to be seen by heads as a complex model.'

Bob Doe, writing in the *TES* on 9 December 1992, quoted the School Teachers' Review Body's claim that 'pay discretion is being used almost exclusively to reward teachers' extra responsibilities, not merit'. Most teachers (82 per cent) received no discretionary payments other than incentive allowances. Of those who did receive such payments those in secondary schools outweighed those in primary schools 2:1. More than half were in London. Whatever the precise working of the system, the widespread use of discretionary payments as a form of accountability is common. In one case the payment was awarded for monitoring unqualified teachers, and in another, four teachers were awarded a lump sum in recognition of extra work and stress with first-year pupils. Out of 2,700 teachers nationally who received incremental allowances in 1992, only about 500 had their pay enhanced because of their classroom performance (*TES*, 9 October 1992).

The whole question is begged about whether it would be possible to reward merit in a consistent and honest way. The profession has always been doubtful about this and, indeed, it is feared that highly subjective judgements might be made about whether a particular teacher's contribution is at a standard where merit should be rewarded with extra pay. The other fear is that such pay could be used to boost salaries.

A report commissioned jointly by the NUT and NAS/UWT and published in summer 1992, was based on interviews with teachers at four primary and five secondary schools. It warned that 'low-achieving pupils might be refused places because their exam results were likely to bring down school averages'. The teachers feared that figures might be manipulated by 'restrictions on school or examination entry'. Such concern was echoed by the National Association of Governors and Managers. The Trade Union Research Unit considered that none of the pupil-related indicators such as exam results, attendance rates and the destination of school-leavers would provide an adequate basis for PRP: 'such superficial measures will appear naive and totally lack credibility with education professionals' (*TES*, 9 October 1992). The NAHT also expressed reservations about the whole concept and practice of PRP. 'Performance indicators must be achievable, professionally acceptable and not so dominating that they narrow the focus and efforts of schools' (*TES*, 9 October 1992).

PERFORMANCE: ASSESSMENT AND APPRAISAL

During August 1991 schoolteacher appraisal became law; every schoolteacher was to be appraised every two years. Appraisal had been a long time ripening. For over two years, sharp comparisons had been made between teachers who were rarely assessed in the formal sense and officers in the armed services, lawyers in most firms, and almost the whole of the Civil Service. For large sections of the population, whether in managerial positions or not, it was customary to have an annual 'progress report'. Few escaped the rigour, real or imagined, of this common practice. It mattered little whether the civil servant liked being assessed or not; the practice continued.

Somehow the formal assessment or appraisal of teachers had been avoided, but for no really good reason. At peripheral discussions when no decisions had to be taken and no individual was being named, there was semantic talk about whether teachers should be so measured. Seminars were held to consider subtle distinctions between assessment and appraisal; one was considered more authoritarian and therefore more threatening than the other. How many 'sensitive' teachers would have their integrity and professional freedom debased by being evaluated? How could such an emotionally 'fragile' group of men and women, who were endlessly committed and giving their all, be made accountable for their actions?

Various questions were asked. What was the percentage of time spent on the various aspects of a teacher's work? How long was spent on preparation, or marking, or contact time? If any machinery made teachers more accountable wouldn't their voluntary contributions suffer? Would the same enthusiasm still go into the debating society, the games programme or the chess club if teachers were worried because the other parts of their job were being assessed?

Just as there was pseudo-philosophical discussion about semantics there was also a comparable comment that teachers made intangible contributions that were beyond measurement and price. There were those who were taken in by neither the philosophical nor the intangible; those who believed that teachers suffered emotional strain like many other people, that their work was no more demanding than most, and that it was high time that the whole nature of their task was investigated, evaluated and made accountable. If it regularly happened to the nurse and to the doctor why should it not happen to the teacher and the head? If stress, strain and anxiety could not be measured, according to the teachers' unions (who were perhaps correct), perhaps a start could be made by looking more carefully at that which was measurable.

In 1989, six local education authorities - Cumbria, Newcastle, Suffolk, Croydon, Somerset and Devon - decided to produce their own pilot schemes anticipating that central government might, in the near future, wish to introduce such measures, and anxious to understand the nature of the task and the associated problems. This innovation was in line with the established principles of the Advisory, Conciliation and Arbitration Service (ACAS).

There soon followed a report of the national steering group's committee: *School Teachers' Appraisal: A National Framework* (DES, 1989a). This explained what had to be done to introduce any such scheme and referred in detail to solutions and experiences of the six pioneer authorities. A distillation of those experiences went into a video called *Appraisal*, which was designed to show how the first schools worked out their own salvation with specific reference to who should be the appraiser, whether the whole school should be appraised before or after the individual appraisals, how to safeguard equal opportunities, and how to reconcile gathering information with complete confidentiality. The conclusion was clear and encouraging. Get everybody together, look at the different ways it has been done in the past, and then work out something that will be effective and applicable to your own situation. At best, and with a little luck and a lot of goodwill, the appraisal can be positive and affirming. How then does it work?

The initial meeting between the appraiser and the appraisee is critical because it is at that meeting that terms of reference are to be set. What is to be the substance of the review? Which parts of the job description, training needs or career development would it be useful to talk about? What information needs to be collected? How should the dialogue be held, and when should a final written statement be completed? Whatever is decided, it should be reviewed after one year.

It is also suggested in the video that a teacher should begin with a self-appraisal, which should contain both a job description and a job specification. Cornwall County Council included this self-appraisal in the advice pack and incorporated a desire to include areas of responsibility, satisfaction or dissatisfaction, and any changes the teacher would recommend to 'improve the performance, morale or general well-being of the school'. Cornwall gives a guide to the dialogue. It should be 'positive, relaxed with a clear unambiguous question to start the dialogue. It should keep to the agenda, always ensuring the appraisee has said everything he wanted to. At the end it should review everything that has been discussed, checking the follow-up, and finally thanking the appraisee.' Once the statement has been written and agreed, only the head, the chief executive officer and the two conducting the dialogue should see it. A teacher who is not satisfied can register his or her disagreement.

The minimum time agreed by the national steering group between the first appraisal and the follow-up amounts to 64 hours in the first year, and is all in directed time. Heads should be appraised by other heads and it was suggested that 50 headteacher-hours would be needed for this.

Obvious problems are revealed. Appraisal will cost money and small schools, like primaries, will find it painful to use their budget for this task. Lack of money for training will affect most aspects of appraisal but perhaps particularly the cause of equal opportunities. In commenting on *School Teachers' Appraisal* the NUT recommends that 'LEAs and schools set targets to ensure that as many women and black teachers as possible receive training as appraisers'. An additional problem came from the use of the line management approach by which only heads, deputy heads and heads of department will appraise those lower down the ladder; the reason is obvious but the results could be deeply divisive. The idea that heads should be appraised by other heads comes under fire from some who believe that other senior members of staff in the same school would be preferable because they would better understand the ethos of the school.

It is still early days with this idea but as Susan Thomas pointed out in her article in *School Management* in February 1992, it is clear that such an exercise will require considerable 'skill, perception and objectivity' on all fronts. It also requires considerable honesty especially in the 'genuine dialogue between appraisee and appraiser', and 'trust and confidence so that this open method of discussion and evaluation can take place'. Without the skills, the honesty, and the trust, the whole exercise of appraisal could become hollow.

The spoken – and often the unspoken – fear is that appraisal will soon be linked with PRP. Many believe that it is the first step on this road. According to George Harris, of the NUT national executive, 'a school is like a company. We, the teachers, are the managers and the governors are the investors. At the end of the day they need to see overall targets, performance figures and balance sheets. What they don't need is the detail of individual appraisal reports.'

Susan Thomas sounded a more characteristic warning: 'It should be a welcome adjunct to good practice and professional growth. Instead it is viewed with a mixture of weary scepticism and, as with the legendary chimera, what you see depends on your point of view.' She headed her article: 'Fear of the first judgement'. Many outside the profession thought it was long overdue.

PARTNERSHIP IN TRAINING

The proposed revolution in the practice of training teachers has of necessity to be based on a working and workable partnership between schools and students and educationists. It cannot succeed unless it is at least that.

Oxford led the way. Here each year 190 postgraduate students are attached to 18 local secondary comprehensive schools. They work for two days a week at first, learn some basic techniques, and become members of staff. The university tutors act in concert with experienced teachers. The students are concentrated in subject pairs in each school with, say, five students and five teachers. Each week these ten meet, together with university tutors and other appropriate members of staff, and consider a whole range of topics, such as discipline and pastoral care. The assignments the student writes usually derive from these seminars and, consequently, are a link between theory and practice. Everybody is happy. Students feel they are receiving training comparable to that of medical students. Staff feel they are rightly involved in the selection and training of new entrants to their profession. University tutors are much closer to the schools and it gives them at once that first-hand experience for the lack of which they have previously been criticized. Pupils are also benefiting, not only from the latest, most up-to-date approaches but from fresh ideas and the regular infusion of young students nearer to their own age. It is altogether a promising and welcome arrangement.

However, it does contain some serious pitfalls. In the 1950s Robin Pedley, an ideological advocate of comprehensive education, feared that if non-selective schools became too large it might be difficult to find a sufficient number of suitable teachers. He believed heads of such schools should be the 'statesmen of the institution' and doubted that enough heads of this calibre existed. There was also doubt about whether a sufficiently large number of 'master teachers' capable of being the mentors of student teachers in their schools existed. There is also the standing query raised about every educational reform: that the necessary funding would have to be found. To hear such objections from the die-hards makes one think that they would even have found economic objections to Abelard lecturing from the steps of Chartres Cathedral. It is as though every trainee teacher needs to be nurtured in a perfect situation before anything can be attempted. The truth is that the good is often preferable to the best; it is usually better to make some start rather than not start at all. But the most important criticism of the Oxford scheme under Professor Pring, Director of the Oxford Department of Educational Studies, is that it virtually destroys the nature of the much criticized university departments of education. One of the main reasons why the Oxford partnership in teacher training has been accepted so swiftly and so warmly is because it effectively neutralizes existing colleges and departments of teacher training. And yet there is a serious fear that such a total revolution could throw the baby out with the bath water. Superficial and trite criticisms of old-style teacher training are easy to find, and many of them are well justified, yet there is much virtue in the institutions and often in the valuable research they carry out. The case for reform is unassailable in the main, but the extreme nature of what followed is more difficult to justify. The main fear in the foreseeable future is that serious philosophical thinking about the task of teacher training will be jettisoned when preparations for entry into the classroom actually move into the schools. This is a sad reflection, because an absence of philosophical thought and perspective runs the risk of allowing originality and innovation to wither or, worse still, to be restricted to the small-mindedness of the school: the parochial looking inwards.

Lynne Marsh, an external examiner for the Cambridge Department of Education's Postgraduate Certificate in Education (PGCE) course made three pertinent comments in an article in the *TES* on 21 February 1992. She recognizes that lecturers already have a 'good working knowledge of the profession' and welcomes their proposed involvement with the schools. She adds the important comment that it would

be impossible for a school to take the leading role in the training
of teachers because schools must be first and foremost concerned
with the education of the pupils in their care. The student teachers
will have to work hard to ensure that their immediate and pressing
concerns to develop their skills as teachers are not damaged.

A little later in the same article, she voices her concern 'that by
putting a student teacher into schools for 80% of their timetable,
their training will become fragmented with no clear direction'.

Pring has no such hang-ups: he has operated an effective scheme
on these lines in the Oxford Department of Educational Studies.
He insists that heads and schools in Oxfordshire want the scheme
for several reasons. First, teachers are undergoing professional
development themselves as they act as mentors. Second, the scheme
provides 'a valuable networking of subject teachers in schools and
professional tutors in the university'. Third, the schools value their
continued link with a university department. Fourth, the students,
whom Pring gives the American medical label of 'interns', 'are
closely supervised and supported and only gradually initiated into
the complex world of the school; by February they are making a
very positive contribution to the schools'.

Pring admits that the scheme depends upon a real partnership
between university and schools. There must be shared values,
shared interest in research, shared selection of schools and shared
development 'of that theoretical perspective of teaching which is
the mark of the professional' (*Sunday Times*, 9 February 1992).

What is clear in the revolutionary changes in teacher training is
that the degree of accountability is quite significantly extended. At
a stroke students have become answerable to schools as well as to
university departments and both institutions have become directly
answerable to each other and to the profession as a whole.

Pring has commented on 'the mark of the professional' and it
is now appropriate to consider the extent to which members of the
profession are accountable to each other.

IS IT A PROFESSION?

Professor Charlton writing in 1965 in *Education in Renaissance
England*, analysed the nature of professions in the sixteenth century and listed seven characteristics:

(1) There should be a relationship of trust and confidence with the client.

(2) An element of public service and duty to the community should be present.

(3) It should relate to an area of well-defined knowledge, to include theoretical knowledge.

(4) A period of training is usually provided, often in an institution.

(5) It is organized and institutionalized to test the competence of members and to maintain it.

(6) It is a social group with its own hierarchy, social life and commitment.

(7) It claims and is accorded status based upon salary, learning acquired at the highest grade, organization and solidarity, code of conduct and professional ethics, and independence.

There is no suggestion that the hallmarks of a profession in the sixteenth century would satisfy all the criteria required for teaching and lecturing at the end of the twentieth, but teaching appears to satisfy most of them to greater or lesser degree. Part of the present situation is related to the professional associations and unions; they are not only part of the professional standing of the teacher, they are also part of his or her accountability within the profession. Within Professor Charlton's criteria they have a relevance to numbers (5), (6) and (7). The real problems arise because there are several competing unions and associations. They have much in common.

They all promote the cause of education, protect the status and interests of teachers, give legal advice and assistance whenever required professionally to act as trustees in any corporate matter connected with their members.

Unions begin to differ in their attitudes to pay negotiations, terms of service and industrial action. It is not appropriate to consider their different stances here, but it is fair to state that the approach to strike action covers the whole range. One union is completely opposed to it in any circumstances and another has chosen to take militant action at every opportunity. I do not intend to pass any value judgement on the position of any of the unions and associations; it is what they stand for and it is their business. This variety does, however, make it difficult to write about a united profession.

To whom are unions answerable? Some, like the NUT, are members of the Trades Union Congress and must obey the rules of that organization. By contrast, the Secondary Heads Association does not choose such an affiliation but it is associated closely with the independent organization of the Headmasters' Conference. Both organizations are accountable to their members.

The particular ways in which they are accountable obviously vary, but they all work through their members in the election of an executive and the appointment of officers, and by holding an annual conference. This structure is buttressed by branch and area meetings, and magazines and special reports. On the face of it, unions represent the democratic process at its best, with members apparently being sovereign. Is this really the case?

'There are trade unionists, once the oppressed, now the tyrants, whose selfish and sectional pretensions need to be bravely opposed,' wrote J.M. Keynes in 1926 (Keynes, 1988). Does this comment have any relevance now? Aside from the fact that not all teacher organizations are technically unions, the passage deserves scrutiny. Who controls the officials? What is the precise way in which the senior officials are appointed? How do members get nominated or elected to the annual conference? What is the indirect influence of the various political parties within the union? What sort of teacher becomes interested in union affairs anyway? There are perfectly acceptable answers to all of these questions and readers can compile the official answers – indeed anyone brought up on television reports by union leaders over the last twenty years would be able to jest about the standard explanations which are always given and have passed into folklore like the interviews with football players after the match. But because the answers are so standardized, the search for the genuine ways in which union affairs become more accountable becomes even more important. What are they trying to hide?

The simple truth is that the majority of teachers only join a union for three reasons: they want someone to represent them in salary negotiations; they want legal protection, especially in case a parent sues them; and they want a cheap mortgage. Those who join the unions for any other reasons are a small minority although they often have a powerful effect on the union as a whole. In the past they have usually been politically motivated, but it would be wrong to assume that they have only been drawn from one political party.

The stark truth is that the lack of commitment on the part of teachers as a whole has left the unions wide open to those seeking to manipulate or influence the educational system for their own ends.

As a result of this distorted representation, unions have become highly political and although their public claim is that they do not represent any one political party, which is correct, it is also true that ginger groups within the individual unions have sometimes had telling effect. It is sad that such small groups of activists only pretend to serve the teachers because it is a convenient platform. Their real loyalty lies outside the teachers' unions.

Accountability in the unions and associations comes at various levels. Officially they are among the most democratic organizations in the land. In the hands of activists they have sometimes become one of the least democratic. For the vast majority of teachers, the whole question of accountability is peripheral to the reasons why they joined in the first place and they have many other and less boring ways of using their free time than as keen union members. For them, accountability goes by default; unions are a relatively unimportant part of their lives.

An evaluation of the rights and wrongs of a decision to go on strike made in 1989 in one union is not my purpose here, but enough teachers felt strongly enough to leave the union concerned in significant numbers. In short, when the leaders, whether salaried or elected, made the decision to take industrial action, the rank and file just left the union. For them it was not a procedural matter to do with motions and voting, but a breach of trust. It is reassuring that when an organization ceases to be accountable it is really signing its own death warrant.

Chapter 8

Maastricht and Education

The Maastricht Treaty is about the political, economic and social cohesion of Europe. Ever since the Treaty of Rome in 1957, European legislation has been moving in the direction of greater integration. Some countries, such as Denmark and the United Kingdom, have clearly expressed their concern about concepts like the United States of Europe, but their reluctance to accept particular provisions has not seriously halted the trend; it has only made those who seek greater integration go more cautiously. Maastricht is the next logical step in the process of bringing Western Europe more closely together. While it has always been claimed that greater togetherness will enhance national interests, and it is difficult to see how it could not, the Treaty also challenges those same national interests. It widens responsibilities because it makes countries more accountable outside their borders for their own national examinations and other educational matters. The French *baccalauréat*, the German *Abitur*, and other countries' internal examinations, are no longer relevant only to people in their own countries but are a part of the direct concerns of all the other partners in the Community because the exams have to be mutually acceptable. In this sense the people who run the examinations are accountable, but it is in a non-economic sense.

The Articles of the Maastricht Treaty which concern education are 57, 126 and 127 and they will now be considered in detail. The first deals with the equivalence of national qualifications. The second is concerned with quality education. The third deals with vocational training.

ARTICLE 57

1. In order to make it easier for persons to take up and pursue activities as self-employed persons, the Council shall . . . issue directives for the mutual recognition of diplomas, certificates and other evidence of formal qualifications.

2. For the same purpose, the Council shall, before the end of the transitional period issue directives for the co-ordination of the provisions laid down by law, regulation or administrative action in Member States concerning the taking up and pursuit of activities as self-employed persons. The Council, acting unanimously on a proposal from the Commission and after consulting the European Parliament, shall decide on directives the implementation of which involves in at least some Member States amendment of the existing principles laid down by law governing the professions with respect to training and conditions of access for natural persons.

3. In the case of the medical and allied and pharmaceutical professions, the progressive abolition of restrictions shall be dependent upon co-ordination of the conditions for their exercise in the various Member States.

This important Article opens up the whole question of comparability of qualifications, which has been one of the biggest obstacles to mobility and association in modern times. The lack of mutual interchange and acceptability of national qualifications has also been a major handicap in various research programmes which have involved people from different countries.

It was partly because there was need for one commonly accepted qualification that the International Baccalaureate (IB) was created and designed. The educational ECU already exists in the IB. The Treaty chose to take the more difficult road of negotiating equivalence.

In the past, one commonly accepted exam currency was the external exams of London University. If London accepted the national qualification as equivalent then all was well, but if it did not, it was necessary to take some other national exam instead. The situation will now be different. Although national exams will be mutually accepted there can be no doubt that the composition of the syllabuses, the methods of assessment, the evaluation and standardization of content will be hard to balance between member countries whose academic traditions are so contrasting.

Accountability is intrinsic to comparability. At the moment, each exam board in the United Kingdom is accountable to the candidates and parents, to the school, to the college or university, and to the country. With the new terms of Maastricht none of these elements will disappear but to them will be added the even more sophisticated dimension of comparability with other exams in Europe. This additional factor will intensify the necessity for effective and reliable methods of accountability. It would be laughable if it was easier to obtain qualifications in one country than in another.

There are far-reaching implications of the move to comparability. It will soon be obvious that a kind of universality in educational acceptance will have developed: what will and what will not be allowed in purely academic terms. The United States of Europe could well become the United Colleges of Europe.

ARTICLE 126: EDUCATION, VOCATIONAL AND YOUTH

1. The Community shall contribute to the development of quality education by encouraging co-operation between Member States and, if necessary, by supporting and supplementing their action, while fully respecting the responsibility of the Member States for the content of teaching and the organisation of education systems and their cultural and linguistic diversity.

2. Community action shall be aimed at:
   - developing the European dimension in education, particularly through the teaching and dissemination of the languages of the Member States;
   - encouraging mobility of students and teachers, inter alia by encouraging the academic recognition of diplomas and periods of study;
   - promoting co-operation between educational establishments;
   - developing exchanges of information and experience on issues common to the education systems of the Member States;
   - encouraging the development of youth exchanges and of exchanges of socio-educational instructors;
   - encouraging the development of distance learning.

3. The Community and the Member States shall foster co-operation with third countries and the competent international organisations in the field of education, in particular the Council of Europe.

4. In order to contribute to the achievement of the objectives referred to in this Article, the Council:
   - consulting the Economic and Social Committee and the Committee of the Regions, shall adopt incentive measures, excluding any harmonisation of the laws and regulations of the Member States;

– acting by a qualified majority on a proposal from the Commission, shall adopt recommendations.

The importance of promoting the culture of the whole of Europe rather than just the heritage of one country is unassailable. The importance of language learning is critical but so also is the transmission of those cultural elements which make up the continent. This can be done through exchanges and co-operation but it needs to be done as something quite specific and deliberate and it is clear that the Treaty is sensitive to the whole question. One hopes that the objectives listed will be achieved without disregarding those national elements which have always existed but which can be even more useful when put inside a continental structure, preferably without too much bureaucracy. What Article 126 is mainly dealing with is the wider view which will give the Community a clearer historical identity.

ARTICLE 127

1. The Community shall implement a vocational training policy which shall support and supplement the action of the Member States, while fully respecting the responsibility of the Member States for the content and organisation of the vocational training.
2. Community action should aim to:
   – facilitate adaptation to industrial changes, in particular through vocational training and retraining;
   – improve initial and continuing vocational training in order to facilitate vocational integration and reintegration into the labour market;
   – facilitate access to vocational training and encourage mobility of instructors and trainees and particularly young people;
   – stimulate co-operation on training between educational or training establishments and firms; develop exchanges of information and experience on issues common to the training organisations in the sphere of vocational training systems of the Member States.
3. The Community and the Member States shall foster co-operation with third countries and the competent international organisations in the sphere of vocational training.
4. The Council . . . after consulting the Economic and Social Committee, shall adopt measures to contribute to the achievement of the objectives referred to in this Article, excluding any harmonisation of the laws and regulations of the Member States.

It was appropriate that the Treaty should acknowledge the centrality of recognizing vocational qualifications. The words of the Article raise all the main points. Most were well known in the member countries already.

In Britain, the National Council for Vocational Qualifications (NCVQ) was set up in 1986 as a new framework for increasing the status of vocational qualifications and to provide a system of continuous education and training throughout a person's working life. It recognized that there were often difficulties in switching from one qualification to another, for a variety of reasons. The NCVQ was not a validating or examining body but an endorsing body certifying that a particular qualification was accredited. It established accreditation of prior learning (APL) or of prior achievement (APA) and arranged for remaining competences to be obtained. The NVQs are placed in a framework according to the area of work and the level they cover. All member states in the European Community have comparable arrangements and all seek to recognize the need to integrate work done 'on the job' and 'off the job' – an emphasis on what people do rather than what they know.

It is exactly this kind of British body which is likely to be established for the Community. It will endorse qualifications, professional and vocational, across national boundaries. All the Articles are about non-economic accountability, if there is really such a thing. If you encourage or accept the comparability of a person's qualifications then you are indirectly influencing that person's marketability. He or she can now work in a different country, can move without restraint, and can, without trying, become an employment risk or asset, but whatever the result, the effect is, in the end, economic.

The Articles in the education section also offer a policy for education in Western Europe. They are the 'nuts and bolts' of what is to happen in the future. They make all member states answerable to each other and therefore accountable at all levels of qualification. It is not prophetic to predict that the advent of an acceptable educational currency is not far distant: an 'Advanced, Bac, Abitur, Examen' run from Geneva and nicknamed the ABAE!

The fear, and the biggest problem, is that the administration that may be created to manage these reforms could be unwieldy, inflexible, slow and dictatorial. Try to imagine a Trinidadian with the Cambridge overseas Higher School Certificate who has a degree from an obscure US university and wants to practise law in Paris. How many troubleshooters would be required to investigate his professional acceptability?

Chapter 9

International Comparisons: USA, France, Sweden

The major reforms in Britain, which have largely come from a wish to make education more accountable, have close parallels elsewhere. The three countries chosen for discussion in this chapter provide contrasts within themselves. The United States is federal, with a system which leaves most decisions and power to the individual state; Michigan, for example, has every right to act differently from California – and does. France, always different, either from brilliance or perversity or both, seeks to retain the traditional intellectual heritage with keen support for modern reforms. It remains a unified country where the state controls, decides and finances education. Sweden – neutral, prosperous, controlled by the Social Democrats for a long continuous period, and with the state having almost total dominance of public institutions – is fully accountable and completely centralized.

THE UNITED STATES OF AMERICA

In the USA, all the money for elementary and secondary schools comes from local or national sources. The majority comes from local sources, including parents, but whatever the source, control and financial auditing are tight. This is usually managed by a large Department of State supervisory service, but in small school systems the superintendent of schools, who is a political nominee, sometimes does it all. Institutions of higher education receive money from federal funds, state funds, and always have a massive and continuous financial appeal from industry and their own alumni.

Accountability became a major part of American educational thinking during the mid-1970s, largely because education was costing so much and people wanted to be sure they were getting value for their money. If this was about control of expenditure it was about making sure money was not being wasted; there was usually no sinister reason lurking behind the arras. By 1974, 32 states had passed some form of legislation about accountability, and although the detail varied there were four common elements: management goals were set up; there was to be assessment of students to monitor whether these goals were being met; cost/ performance analyses were to be made regularly to justify programmes; and regular evaluation of professional personnel was to be undertaken. Twenty years later, on the other side of the Atlantic, the same objectives are being tackled. Some of the American experiments in accountability are now being monitored in Britain.

One of the most interesting is the voucher system. The idea behind this was to give parents an educational allowance for each child, letting them choose the school at which to spend it. On the face of it, this seemed simple, and contained a form of accountability through parents exercising their right of choice. It was market-place economics applied to education. And yet it had some obvious flaws. There was no easy way of ensuring that children would be racially mixed, or that children from certain socioeconomic groups would mix at all, or that the weakest school, in whatever way that weakness was being expressed, would have to close by not having enough patrons to make it viable.

At Alum Rock in California, the US Office of Economic Opportunity supported an experiment in several schools willing to try out a voucher scheme. Six schools, and later another seven, were designated as voucher schools and each was subdivided into minischools with different emphases. For example, one offered a traditional pattern, one was based upon daily living, and one with television sets and a geodesic dome was called School 2000. Early evaluation soon showed that the major changes were in the roles of the staff rather than in parents or children. Teachers had more autonomy and more control over their resources; it transformed their attitudes. Another result was that all the voucher schools suffered a reduction in their achievement scores compared with non-voucher schools. The evaluation of the report by the Rand Corporation analysed in *Social Foundations of Education* (Miller, 1978) concluded that the experiment did not test economic competition, the role of private schools or communication with parents. On the basis of this report no other areas wanted to try out the voucher idea and it died. Even in Alum Rock it was seriously modified.

What the voucher plan had sought to do was to improve performance in schools by making them accountable to parents. It tried to apply the cost/benefit approach in industry to a school's instructional programme. What happened was that academic standards went down and schools cost more money.

Another example in Michigan was reported and assessed by Jerome Murphy and David Cohen in *Accountability in Education – The Michigan Experience* (1974). This was not a voucher system but one which sought to introduce accountability in other ways. The difficulties were considerable. The motivations of all those involved were so different as to be in opposition to each other. Some saw the scheme as a way of reducing costs; others believed it was the golden opportunity to finance long-needed reforms. The different attitudes of such groups caused irreconcilable conflict. The publication of test results often set off such antagonism that much good was at once devalued. Some tests concerned technical issues which were not suitable for public debate nor were they, in some cases, capable of reliable measurement. It was, however, the aspiration to hold school districts accountable for improvement in pupil achievement which foundered on the rocks of politics. Where results declined the district stood to lose millions of dollars. Opposition was enormous, especially in Detroit, and the state legislature gave way and waived the requirement. Murphy and Cohen asked: 'Without such a penalty how can a system of accountability work?' It is perhaps the most telling insight into the permanent effectiveness of plans for accountability anywhere. Would such a sharp conclusion be made to some aspects of comparable schemes in this country? Does it need the withdrawal of funds to make accountability in education work?

It was during the Nixon years in the 1970s that the concept of accountability in education began to spread. It was closely associated with increased emphasis on testing and on the power of the educational expert. To simplify a long and complicated debate which stretched over several years, the argument ran along the following lines. Research had shown that differences in school achievement bore little significant relation to differences in resources. What was needed was an increase in professional expertise, especially in careers education: 'The transition we manage least well in our society is that of the young person leaving the world of school for the world of work' (Murphy and Cohen, 1974).

Leon Lessinger in *Every Kid a Winner* (1971) suggested that the community control movement which wanted to restore control of schools to members of the local community was a threat to the quality of education. He argued that the average member of the community does not have the necessary expertise and experience to make correct educational decisions. Although he recognized that schools must be responsive to the public he believed that this was best done by the schools reporting their accomplishments and failures. 'This public accounting of the results of schooling was the heart of the accountability movement.' It is seen as a matter of quality of education expressed in non-financial terms and yet having financial implications. It is not irrelevant to see it as an economic question, but at the start of the accountability movement the financial element was not central although it was intrinsic. These particular advocates emphasized traditional classroom methods, but elsewhere in the US there were equally strong supporters of more liberal open-classroom approaches. There were thus two sharply drawn sides: the accountability quarter and the reforming quarter.

An exact comparison with the situation in Britain is not possible because two sides do not exist. There is also a difference in official reaction here when moves towards increased accountability are seriously challenged. What usually happens in Britain is that the reforms are gradually modified but not abolished. The protagonists' position in Britain does not become more deeply entrenched when they are attacked. Consequently, the process of constant revision usually means that at least some of the original idea remains and that large numbers of people have shared in the modification and become identified with it.

SWEDEN

The contrast with the USA is total. Sweden's educational system is controlled by the state. It has a hierarchical structure but no part of this detracts from the power of the state in spite of much decentralization at all levels.

The Riksdag makes the major educational policy decisions on legislation, finance and general organization. These are translated into workable action by the Ministry of Education and Cultural Affairs, which in turn leaves implementation to the National Board of Education. This last body is an executive with members appointed by the government from all political parties, employee and employer organizations, municipalities and county councils. It deals with curricular matters, research and development, in-service training, and the evaluation of school work and budget requests. These final two items give the Board a permanent accountability function.

The instrument which is used most powerfully for state control of education is the fixing of the state grant both for the whole country and for each individual municipality. This is why the Riksdag is able to control, in detail, what happens throughout the whole system. There is little in Sweden which does not depend upon state money, and national and local initiatives all derive from it. If money for a project is not allocated in the budget, the project does ʹ not happen.

Within the Board there are four departments: for compulsory schooling, upper schooling, adult education, and administration. There is also a separate audit section which is directly responsible to the senior officials, called the Directorate. Control comes from the top of the pyramid.

Next in the structure is the county education board and in the organization at this level is included a secretariat headed by the county inspector of schools. These inspectors have many tasks which derive from ensuring that current regulations are complied with. These could include almost anything to do with education but the inspectors' role always includes the appointment of heads, training, and the inspection of schools. They have been described as the 'eyes' of the service and they clearly have considerable accountability functions in their work of inspection.

The next tier is the local education committee which meets once or twice every month. It is responsible for the direct political management of schools. The committee tries to ensure that goals are achieved and that 'uniform and equal standards are maintained within the school system' (Stenholm, 1984). It appoints the chief education officer, considers building requests and budget submissions, and constantly updates the guidelines for the allocation of funds to schools. Education committees often have to agree with directives from the national and the municipal funding agencies. They are, in short, tightly controlled on every financial matter.

It is apparent even in this abbreviated description of the Swedish structure that there are many policy-making committees and that these greatly slow down the speed with which reforms can take place. What it does mean, however, is that everything is most carefully considered, and that time, even if it is the time caused by bureaucratic delay, tends to increase the possibility of effective accountability.

There is an important distinction which the Swedish system illustrates: the separation, for the most part, of financial responsibility from quality. The state assumes the greater share of financial responsibility, but it is the municipal authorities which have the last word in determining quality. What this means in practice is that every piece of reform has a double check – one for money and one for quality. By implication, the various people in the system must get on if a new idea is to be put into practice.

The best example of this is the introduction of comprehensive education: Sweden was the first country in Europe to initiate such a reform. The ruling Social Democratic Party championed the change most strongly, believing that all students should be enrolled in one school instead of being divided into three or more groups, each labelled differently at the secondary stage. In this example the centralized system worked in favour of reform and so it was possible to implement the decision. It would be possible to argue that the unwieldy bureaucracy only exists to delay those changes about which there is disagreement. When the majority speaks with one voice change is easier. The other great advantage of the centralized system is that the level of accountability it is possible to employ considerably reduces the amount of money which has to be spent or might be wasted. In other countries that are not so centralized, the introduction of comprehensive education has often been more costly. Sweden is an interesting example because it suggests that a centralized system can increase the possibility of greater and more effective accountability.

FRANCE

'Ce qui n'est pas clair n'est pas français.'

Napoleon built accountability into the structure of the state and it still remains at the centre of the system. There continue to be inspectors with powers to assess, correct and examine work, teachers and the curriculum. Expenditure is still tightly audited and accounted for in detail. People within the system know exactly what is expected of them and, perhaps most importantly, what is not. For example, it is the *surveillant* who is responsible for discipline in the playground and the teacher is not paid to do that job; both people know their roles and their responsibilities. Much the same applies to the financial arrangements in French education, and this has not altered just because socialism has had a significant influence since the late 1960s. France has transformed education but the methods of regulating it have remained updated versions of their traditional patterns. France represents a country which has a time-honoured discipline of accountability. Sometimes this has been a restrictive influence on the consideration of new ideas – like the slowness in implementing the reforms championed by the students in 1968. Depending upon your point of view, this restriction was an advantage or a disadvantage. For those who believed that the rioters were in error, the strictness of the financial restraint, which acted as a delaying mechanism, might give time for the hotheads to come to their senses. Alternatively, such delay could be seen as a deliberate trick to put off taking action so that the protesters lost heart. Accountability has been central to French education for nearly 200 years, whether times are quiet or revolutionary.

The most recent reforms make the primary school the universal stage of training for all children. Secondary schools have also radically changed, and the first four years in both the *lycées* and the colleges now include all children, irrespective of abilities, and are compulsory. The three upper forms have four sections – classical, modern, technical and artistic – and students move into the one to which they are best suited; this can clearly lead to considerable undisclosed selection. However the sections are graded, they have somehow managed to retain their old identity and ambience.

The financing of education has always been clearly structured. *Lycées* are national institutions and maintained from state funds. Colleges are financed by municipalities. Teachers are paid by the state. Examinations have greatly changed but their names are the same and they are still monitored and directed centrally by the inspectorate as they always have been. Higher education is also funded by the state but the changes in the nature of the students, both intellectual and social, have resulted in the creation of three stages. The first stage, for the years 18 to 20, consists of preparatory studies for the professions, training teachers for technical and normal schools, and training for technicians of intermediate grades. The second stage, for those between 20 and 21, includes those working for first degrees (*licences*) in the arts, sciences, medicine and law faculties. The third stage consists of the *Grandes Ecoles*, those special institutions which provide France with her intellectual leaders, experts and top-flight administrators. Only students possessing *licences* may start this course. The *agrégation*, which had previously been a special state examination, will now be included in the third stage of the university. This third stage also includes those who are doing research. What France has tried to do is to provide equality of opportunity in education, satisfy the demands of the students for a more flexible and modern approach, and contain all these changes in the well-tried framework of sound financing.

In 1986 the Organization for Economic Co-operation and Development (OECD) in a report on innovation policy in France, wrote that 'the centralisation of the French system has been held to reinforce its rigidity'. A philosophical discussion of this comment may not seem profitable but it might be relevant to make a comparison with Sweden. Both countries' systems are centralized but they are nevertheless very different. Clearly, national temperament and culture are in strong contrast. In basic geographical terms France is much larger than Sweden and it might be argued that accountability is easier to achieve in smaller countries; it could conversely be argued that the long tradition of order and organization in France more than compensates for any apparent handicap caused by the country being large. Perhaps the political parties in the two countries provide a clearer insight. Sweden has majority rule by the Social Democratic Party, which has provided the stability which comes from an awareness of the needs of government, especially those of a financial nature. France is quite different, with a wide range of parties, coalitions, groupings and internal alliances; there is rarely a consensus, and even more rarely a steady state in any sense. In default of political serenity, France has traditionally relied upon familiar patterns of administrative government. In this way the French have been forced to live with a form of governmental rigidity which comes in part from the centralized nature of the state but also from the need to offer some counterbalancing stability to the uncertain political party situation. This very rigidity includes all the well-tried mechanisms of accountability in financing, the inspectorate and the curriculum for which the country is famous. In many aspects of French life Napoleon is still at work, nowhere more so than in education.

IS THERE VALUE IN THE COMPARISON?

Edmund King, in his foreword to Dr Halls's *Society, Schools and Progress in France* (1965), comments that education is now 'a publicly regulated, publicly financed activity'. He argues that the state 'will assume a mounting responsibility for the allocation of funds' and that 'everyone's education is likely to be to the advantage of everyone else in the long run'. In these two statements, actually on the same page, Dr King not only hints at an accountability but also at the critical importance of realizing that no country can consider an education policy, or any other for that matter, in isolation.

The two opposite ends of the range of choices are represented by the USA's complete devolution expressed through local school boards, and Sweden and France's centrally run school systems. In the latter, rules are enforced about all aspects of school organization, especially the financial. Britain fits midway between these extremes although the diminution in the power of LEAs, the imposition of a National Curriculum, and the creation of grant-maintained schools have significantly changed the place of Britain on this imaginary scale.

There can be no doubt that the way this government and indeed all governments are able to increase expenditure on education is through financial leverage. The power of the LEAs is limited and now reduced by controlling the money available. The attraction of becoming a grant-maintained school was not only the increased freedom which would result but also the increased money. This has been the case not only in Britain; it applies in all countries, including those highlighted in this chapter. Sweden for example withdrew state aid to private schools and, at a stroke, they became almost extinct.

Britain is moving quite decisively towards a more centralized system. The change became more obvious, according to Heidenheimer, Heclo and Adams in *Comparative Public Policy*, 'around 1900 [when] the British Education Ministry acted more as a central paymaster than as a ministry' (Heidenheimer *et al.*, 1990, p. 28). What the book does not suggest is that the roles may in the future be merged in an educational world where those concerned are responsible for not only the intellectual but also the financial implications of their actions. The examples in this chapter emphasize the fact that educators are now accountable whatever country they work in and whatever political structure the country chooses to adopt. Accountability is now part of every system. It is not a clever way of describing one particular method; it is universal.

Bibliography

Ball, C. and Eggins, H. (eds) (1992) *Higher Education in the 1990's*. Milton Keynes: Open University Press.

Becher, T. and Kogan, M. (1987) *Calling Britain's Universities to Account*. London: Education Reform Group.

Becher, T. and Maclure, S. (1978) *Accountability in Education*. Slough: NFER.

Bligh, D. (1982) *Accountability or Freedom for Teachers*. Guildford: Society for Research in Higher Education.

Cave, R. and Cave, J. (1985) *Teacher Appraisal*. Newmarket: Gazeley.

Charlton, K. (1965) *Education in Renaissance England*. London: Routledge and Kegan Paul.

Coopers & Lybrand (1988) *Local Management in Schools*.

Cosin, B., Flude, M. and Hales, M. (eds) (1990) *School, Work, and Equality*. London: Hodder and Stoughton, in association with the Open University.

Crouch, C. and Dore, R. (1990) *Corporatism and Accountability*. Oxford: Clarendon Press.

Crowther-Hunt, (1983) In M. Shattock (ed.), *The Structure and Governance of Higher Education*. Guildford: Society for Research in Higher Education.

DES (1987) *Higher Education: Meeting the Challenge*. London: HMSO.

DES (1989a) *School Teachers' Appraisal: A National Framework*. London: HMSO.

DES (1989b) *The English Polytechnics: An HMI Commentary*. London: HMSO.

DES, *Annual Reports of the HMI: 1989-90, 1990-91, 1991-92*. London: HMSO.

DES (1992a) *How Is Your Child Doing at School? A Parent's Guide to Tests and Reports for 7 year olds*. London: HMSO.

DES (1992b) *How Is Your Child Doing at School? A Parent's Guide to Tests and Reports for 14 year olds*. London: HMSO.

DES (1992c) *Diversity and Choice: A New Framework for Schools*. London: HMSO.

Douglas, B. (1989) *Implementing Local Management in Schools*. Sheffield City Polytechnic Department of Educational Management. Harlow: Longman.

Eisner, E. (1985) *The Art of Educational Evaluation*. London: Falmer.

Halls, W.D. (1965) *Society, Schools and Progress in France*. Oxford: Pergamon.

Hans, N. (1980) *Comparative Education*. London: Routledge and Kegan Paul.

Harding, P. (1987) *A Guide to Governing Schools*. London: Harper.

Heidenheimer, A.J., Heclo, H. and Adams, C.T. (1990) *Comparative Public Policy*. New York: St Martin's Press.

Howell, D.A. (1989) *The Educational Insiders*. Harlow: Longman.

Hume, B. (1990) 'Building Bridges', speech at North of England Conference.

Jefferson, T. and Grimshaw, R. (1984) *Controlling the Constable, Police Accountability in England and Wales*. London: Fred Muller, in association with the Cobden Trust.

Jones, D. (1986) *Accountability and Budgets in Colleges*. Guildford: Society for Research in Higher Education.

Kedourie, E. (1988) *Diamonds and Glass*. London: Centre for Policy Studies.

Keynes, J.M. (1988) *Economic Consequences of the Peace*. London: Penguin.

Kogan, M. (1986) *Education Accountability*. London: Hutchinson.

Lacey, C. and Lawton, D. (1981) *Issues in Evaluation and Accountability*. London: Methuen.

Lawlor, S. (1988) *Away with LEA's*. London: Centre for Policy Studies.

Lawrence, I. (1992) *Power and Politics at the Department of Education and Science*. London: Cassell.

Lello, J. (1964) *The Official View of Education*. Oxford: Pergamon.

Lello, J. (1979) *Accountability in Education*. London: Ward Lock Educational.

Lessinger, L.M. and Tyler, R.W. (1971) *Every Kid a Winner*. New York: Simon and Schuster.

Loukes, H., Wilson, J. and Cowell, B. (1983) *Education*. Oxford: Martin Robertson.

Lowe, C. (1988) *The Education Reform Act 1988*. Leicester: Secondary Heads Association.

McCormick, R. (ed.) (1982) *Calling Education to Account*. London: Heinemann, in association with the Open University.

MacDonald, B. (1979) *Hard Times – a Review*. Norwich: University of East Anglia.

Messer, J. (1990) *LMS in Action*. Basingstoke: Macmillan Education.

Miller, H.L. (1978) *Social Foundations of Education*. New York and London: Holt, Rinehart and Winston.

Moberly, W. (1949) *Crisis in the University*. London: SCM.

Montgomery, D. and Hadfield, N. (1989) *Practical Teacher Appraisal*. London: Kogan Page.

Murphy, J. and Cohen, D. (1974) *Accountability in Education – The Michigan Experience*. The Public Interest, Number 36. Ann Arbor, Michigan.

Normanton, E.L. (1966) *The Accountability and Audit of Governments*. Manchester: Manchester University Press.

OECD (1986) *Innovation Policy*. Paris.

Ollerenshaw, K. (1978) *Accountability and the Curriculum*. London: College of Preceptors.

Rawlings, J.J. (1989) *Accountability Not Negotiable*. Accra: Ghana Information Services.

Scott, P. (1984) *The Crisis of the University*. London: Croom Helm.

Simey, M. (1988) *Democracy Re-discovered*. London: Zwan.

Sockett, H. (ed.) (1980) *Accountability in the English Educational System*. London: Hodder and Stoughton.

Spring, J. (1990) *The American School 1642–1990*. Harlow: Longman.

Stenholm, B. (1984) *The Swedish School System*. Stockholm: Swedish Institute.

Stephens, M.D. (ed.) (1989) *Universities, Education, and the National Economy*. London: Routledge.

Taylor, F. (1983) *Accountability in Education*. Norwich: Anglian Regional Management Centre.

Thomas, H. (1990) *Education Costs and Performance*. London: Cassell.

Wagner, R.B. (1989) *Accountability in Education*. London: Routledge.

Warnock, M. (1989) *Universities: Knowing Our Minds* (in series, Counter Blasts, number 8). London: Chatto.

Whitfield, R. (1976) *Curriculum Planning, Teaching and Education Accountability*. Birmingham: Department of Educational Enquiry, University of Aston in Birmingham.

Wragg, E.C. (1987) *Teacher Appraisal*. Basingstoke: Macmillan Education.

Index